Madame Bovary
Shmoop Learning Guide

    Chew on Dissatisfaction
    Theme of Freedom and Confinement 45
    Questions About Freedom and Confinement 45
    Chew on Freedom and Confinement 46
    Theme of Foolishness and Folly 46
    Questions About Foolishness and Folly 46
    Chew on Foolishness and Folly 46
    Theme of Love 46
    Questions About Love 47
    Chew on Love 47
    Theme of Women and Femininity 47
    Questions About Women and Femininity 47
    Chew on Women and Femininity 47
    Theme of Wealth 48
    Questions About Wealth 48
    Chew on Wealth 48
    Theme of Appearances 48
    Questions About Appearances 48
    Chew on Appearances 49
    Theme of Repression 49
    Questions About Repression 49
    Chew on Repression 49
    Theme of Art and Culture 49
    Questions About Art and Culture 49
    Chew on Art and Culture 50
Quotes 50
    Dissatisfaction Quotes 50
    Freedom and Confinement Quotes 52
    Foolishness and Folly Quotes 54
    Love Quotes 57
    Women and Femininity Quotes 59
    Wealth Quotes 61
    Appearances Quotes 64
    Repression Quotes 66
    Art and Culture Quotes 68
Plot Analysis 70
    Classic Plot Analysis 70
    Booker's Seven Basic Plots Analysis: Tragedy 72
    Three Act Plot Analysis 73
Study Questions 73
Characters 74
    All Characters 74
        Emma Bovary Character Analysis 74
        Emma Bovary Timeline and Summary 75
        Charles Bovary Character Analysis 79
        Charles Bovary Timeline and Summary 79
        Monsieur Homais Character Analysis 81

Monsieur Homais Timeline and Summary	81
Rodolphe Boulanger de la Huchette Character Analysis	82
Rodolphe Boulanger de la Huchette Timeline and Summary	83
Léon Dupuis Character Analysis	83
Léon Dupuis Timeline and Summary	84
Monsieur Lheureux Character Analysis	85
Berthe Bovary Character Analysis	86
Madame Homais Character Analysis	86
Character Roles	86
Character Clues	88

Literary Devices ... 89
Symbols, Imagery, Allegory ... 89
Setting ... 89
Narrator Point of View ... 90
Genre ... 90
Tone ... 91
Writing Style ... 91
What's Up With the Title? ... 92
What's Up With the Epigraph? ... 92
What's Up With the Ending? ... 92

Did You Know? ... 93
Trivia ... 93
Steaminess Rating ... 93
Allusions and Cultural References ... 93

Best of the Web ... 94
Movie or TV Productions ... 94
Videos ... 95
Images ... 95
Websites ... 95

Madame Bovary
Shmoop Learning Guide

About this Learning Guide

Shmoop Will Make You a Better Lover*
*of Literature, History, Poetry, Life...

Our lively learning guides are written by experts and educators who want to show your brain a good time. Shmoop writers come primarily from Ph.D. programs at top universities, including Stanford, Harvard, and UC Berkeley.

Want more Shmoop? We cover literature, poetry, bestsellers, music, US history, civics, biographies (and the list keeps growing). Drop by our website to see the latest.

www.shmoop.com

©2010 Shmoop University, Inc. All Rights Reserved.
Talk to the Labradoodle... She's in Charge.

Madame Bovary
Shmoop Learning Guide

Table of Contents

Introduction 4
    In a Nutshell 4
    Why Should I Care? 4

Summary 5
    Book Summary 5
    Part I, Chapter One 7
    Part I, Chapter Two 7
    Part I, Chapter Three 8
    Part I, Chapter Four 9
    Part I, Chapter Five 9
    Part I, Chapter Six 10
    Part I, Chapter Seven 11
    Part I, Chapter Eight 12
    Part I, Chapter Nine 13
    Part II, Chapter One 15
    Part II, Chapter Two 16
    Part II, Chapter Three 16
    Part II, Chapter Four 17
    Part II, Chapter Five 18
    Part II, Chapter Six 19
    Part II, Chapter Seven 21
    Part II, Chapter Eight 22
    Part II, Chapter Nine 23
    Part II, Chapter Ten 24
    Part II, Chapter Eleven 25
    Part II, Chapter Twelve 27
    Part II, Chapter Thirteen 29
    Part II, Chapter Fourteen 30
    Part II, Chapter Fifteen 32
    Part III, Chapter One 33
    Part III, Chapter Two 34
    Part III, Chapter Three 35
    Part III, Chapter Four 35
    Part III, Chapter Five 35
    Part III, Chapter Six 37
    Part III, Chapter Seven 39
    Part III, Chapter Eight 40
    Part III, Chapter Nine 42
    Part III, Chapter Ten 43
    Part III, Chapter Eleven 43

Themes 45
    Theme of Dissatisfaction 45
    Questions About Dissatisfaction 45

Madame Bovary
Shmoop Learning Guide

Introduction

In a Nutshell

You've probably heard of Gustave Flaubert's *Madame Bovary*. Maybe it's because you caught a re-run of some old French movie version of it super late one night, or perhaps you've seen a beat-up copy of it lying around from your parents' school days. Why is it so famous? Well, first of all, the book made a huge splash when it was first published. The novel originally appeared in installments in a magazine called *La Revue de Paris* in 1856, which caught the eye of the censors. As a result, Flaubert was put on trial in January of 1857 for obscenity; the novel seemed too risqué for the tastes of the government. The trial actually had the opposite effect to the one the authorities had hoped for; after Flaubert was acquitted, the book became a smash hit.

After its tempestuous birth, *Madame Bovary* continued to make waves in the literary scene. It's seen as one of the best examples of the Realist novel (see more in "Genre"), and its influence was strongly felt in the decades that followed. In the novel, Flaubert takes us to a level of intimacy and familiarity with his characters that was unimaginable before he came along; even if we don't like the characters or don't think they're doing the right thing, we still feel incredibly close to them.

Even today, Flaubert's masterpiece is still going strong. In 2007, a book called *The Top Ten* polled 125 famous authors for their top 10 books of all time and constructed a master list from all of their input. *Madame Bovary* came in second place, a most impressive finish, only behind *Anna Karenina*.

Why Should I Care?

Sex and the Provincial Village: Take One

The year is 1857. Carrie Bradshaw, Charlotte York, Miranda Hobbes, and Samantha Jones are in a small village in France. Lights, camera, action!

CARRIE: Boy, this sure ain't New York.

CHARLOTTE: I like it – it's quaint. Look at those chickens!

MIRANDA: Quaint? Quaint? I need wireless.

SAMANTHA: Hmm, look at the tight pants on that farm boy.

CARRIE: Where are the stores?

CHARLOTTE: Oh dear – where's the restroom?

Madame Bovary
Shmoop Learning Guide

MIRANDA: *Where is the $#(*&$! wireless!*

SAMANTHA: Farm boy! Come back! Farm boy! Don't be scared!

CARRIE: *(voice over)* It was then that I realized that rural France and I weren't meant to be together. You can take a girl out of New York, but you can't take the New York out of the girl.

Luckily for Carrie and her friends, *Sex and the Provincial Village* isn't happening any time soon. However, their frustrations in Yonville-l'Abbaye might not be so dissimilar to those of Emma Bovary. Though Emma's not actually from a big city, she feels like her real place is in Paris, which at her time considered itself the center of the universe. Being in Tostes and Yonville severely cramps her style.

Unlike the other women in the book, Emma is concerned with fashion, sex, and excitement. However, in the world that she lives in, simply going from man to man in the quest for perfect happiness is not an option; Emma is restricted by polite society's rules and by her marriage to Charles, and her retail therapy is constantly threatened by debt and ruination. All the same, we can see the similarities between Emma and her savvy New York descendants – Emma, perhaps, is not just a nineteenth century woman stuck in the wrong town and the wrong marriage, but a very modern woman stuck in the wrong century.

Summary

Book Summary

Charles Bovary is a pretty dull guy. He has an average career, no ambition, and has already been through an unhappy marriage of convenience to a harpy-like widow. With wife # 1 out of the way, however, he's free to marry again – and soon enough, he finds a gorgeous, exciting girl named Emma Rouault.

Emma, a convent-educated farm girl with a head full of romantic fantasies and ideals, is willing to do anything to get off her father's farm, so she and Charles end up married in short order. The couple moves first to a tiny town called Tostes, where Charles, a kind of low-grade doctor, sets up a medical practice. Soon enough, though, Emma is bored, sick of Charles, and incredibly depressed.

The couple attends a ball given by a local aristocrat; there, Emma gets a glimpse of the opulent lifestyle she longs for. Her depression worsens after this life-changing event, and the young couple moves to a slightly larger town, Yonville-l'Abbaye, in an attempt to make her feel better.

Emma, who is pregnant during the move, is slightly soothed by her friendship with another young person, Léon Dupuis, a clerk in Yonville. Léon lives with the family of Monsieur Homais, the town pharmacist. Monsieur Homais also quickly befriends the Bovarys for his own reasons.

After Emma has her baby, Berthe, she and Léon grow even closer. Slowly, they both realize

Madame Bovary
Shmoop Learning Guide

that they're in love – but they're both too shy to do anything about it. Léon moves away to Paris to study, and Emma, left alone, falls back into a slump.

However, her unhappiness doesn't last too long this time – she quickly meets another handsome bachelor, Rodolphe Boulanger. He's quite a womanizer, and he decides to take Emma as his mistress. It doesn't take much convincing to win her over, and Emma quickly succumbs to the temptations of adultery.

Emma starts taking out huge loans from a local merchant, and quickly slides into debt. However, she doesn't care; all that matters to her is Rodolphe. They have a tumultuous relationship for two years, but it eventually comes to a dramatic stop. Rodolphe is bored with Emma, and he abandons her just as they're supposed to run away together. He goes the super-wussy route of writing her a break-up letter, and doesn't even deliver it himself.

This devastates Emma. She goes into shock and her health declines rapidly. Charles doesn't know what to do; mostly, he just prescribes odd and useless medications. The Bovary family's finances get even worse, and Charles is forced to take out additional loans. Emma slowly starts to recover. As a treat, Monsieur Homais suggests that Charles take the little lady to the opera in Rouen, the nearest city. It turns out to be a fateful trip.

At the theatre, Charles and Emma happen to run into Léon, who has finished law school and moved to Rouen. He's become more worldly and is no longer afraid of Emma. They fling themselves into a passionate affair. She grows craftier and craftier, and figures out different schemes to visit the city to see her lover.

However, after a while, even this affair starts to peter out. Emma's money troubles get worse and worse, as does her relationship with Léon. One day when she returns to Yonville, she discovers that she owes an incredibly huge sum of money, and can't possibly pay it back. Disaster!

Emma rushes around, attempting to borrow cash from everyone she knows. The answer everywhere is "no." She tries Léon, to no avail; she even goes back to Rodolphe to ask him to take her back (and pay off her debt), but has no luck with anyone. Desperate, afraid to tell Charles, and completely hopeless, Emma gives in to her despair and poisons herself by taking arsenic. She dies a truly gruesome death, as her friends and family look on in horror.

After Emma's death, things go even more downhill for Charles and little Berthe. They're totally broke. And their finances are made even worse by the fact that Charles, who's still in love with his dead wife despite the proof of her adultery, refuses to sell any of Emma's extravagant possessions. He dies, poverty-stricken and lonely. Berthe is sent to live with her grandmother, who then dies as well. The young girl finally ends up living with a poor aunt, working as a child laborer in a cotton mill.

Ironically, the only character to achieve a happy ending is the determined, obnoxious, over-ambitious, and undeserving apothecary, Monsieur Homais.

Madame Bovary
Shmoop Learning Guide

Part I, Chapter One

- A nameless first-person narrator (never heard from again after this chapter) recounts the day young Charles Bovary appeared at school.
- Charles is an embarrassed, rusticated, slow, and bewildered rural fellow. Also, he's a *total* fashion victim.
- Charles has some difficulty managing his tragically ugly hat; the teacher and the other boys all mock him.
- The class gets even rowdier, and the teacher assigns some lines to punish them. Things quiet down, though Charles is attacked with surreptitious spitballs.
- The other boys observe the newcomer carefully. He's not terribly bright, but he's a hard worker. Next, we get some background on the Bovary family: Charles's dad is a boastful but unsuccessful businessman who pretty much fails to support his family. His poor mom, whose money sustained her husband through his attempts at finding a career, is embittered, peevish, and obsessed with her son.
- Charles received a half-hearted education, but spent most of his childhood left to his own devices, running barefoot around the village and chasing turkeys (Whoohoo!).
- Despite his lackluster upbringing, Charles's parents hope that he'll make a name for himself. After a pretty average, unmemorable time at school, they enroll him in medical school, where he begins to appreciate the finer things in life: the stereotypical temptations of wine, women, and song.
- After failing his exams once, then cramming like crazy and passing a second time, Charles manages to get certified as an *officier de santé* (health officer). This is kind of like a junior doctor; it's a guy who's not a real doctor, but is allowed to practice medicine.
- Mama Bovary is happy. She sets Charles up in a nearby town, Tostes, then marries him off to a wealthy, needy widow. You've got to feel bad for the guy.

Part I, Chapter Two

- The young "doctor" is awakened in the night by a call from a patient; someone at a farm called Les Bertaux outside the town has a broken leg that needs to be set. It's agreed that Charles will head out to take care of the patient at moonrise.
- Until then, Charles lies awake, dreading the medical debacle about to unfold. We've already figured out that he's not exactly the sharpest knife in the drawer, and he doesn't feel too confident about his healing powers. We have to admit, we're nervous for him and his patient, too…seriously, would *you* want this guy operating on your broken leg?
- Les Bertaux turns out to be a nice piece of real estate. Monsieur Rouault, the farmer/patient, is obviously pretty well off. A widower, he takes care of the family farm with the help of his young daughter. Said daughter lets Charles in and takes him up to the patient.
- Monsieur Rouault is a good-natured man, and his fracture also proves to be somewhat good-natured; it's a totally clean break, and Charles starts to feel confident again. He cheers up his patient, and competently takes care of the injury.
- In the meanwhile, the daughter, Emma, attempts to make herself useful by sewing some

Madame Bovary
Shmoop Learning Guide

- padding, but she turns out to be a bad seamstress. Her ineptitude doesn't matter, though – Charles is quite taken by her dainty appearance (she's a total babe). As the three of them go downstairs to have a bite to eat, the young doctor takes a better look at the young daughter.
- Charles (and we) get to know Emma a little better. She hates country living, and doesn't seem quite content with her life. We're not sure if Charles notices this. What he *does* notice is that she is really beautiful. She's got gorgeous brown eyes, full lips, carefully arranged black hair, and rosy cheeks. Someone's got a crush…
- Charles keeps visiting Les Bertaux, supposedly to check in with his patient, but really to see Emma. His irritable/irritating wife finds out that Emma is something of a fine young lady, having received a fancy education at a convent, and is upset by the idea that Charles is in love with the girl. She makes Charles promise not to visit Les Bertaux anymore.
- Charles's first wife is not long in this world. Some bad financial news emerges (it turns out she was lying to the Bovarys about how much money she had in the first place, and Mom and Pop Bovary freak out big time), and the distraught woman actually collapses and dies. Charles is now free, although he *does* feel a little sad, since she loved him.

Part I, Chapter Three

- Charles's half-hearted mourning doesn't last too long. Monsieur Rouault shows up the day after the funeral to deliver his payment for the medical treatment, and also to give his condolences. He encourages Charles to visit Les Bertaux again, which he does, happily.
- Monsieur Rouault cheers Charles up, and he quickly begins to forget about his dead wife. In the weeks that follow, things start to look up for Charles. He discovers that he likes living without his wife – he can decide when and what he wants to eat, and doesn't have to explain himself to anyone. Furthermore, her death was actually good for business, since all the townspeople feel bad for him.
- Charles keeps up his visits to Les Bertaux. One day, he encounters Emma alone. She convinces him to have a drink by saying that she'll have one, too. She pours herself a few drops of liqueur, but in order to taste it, she throws back her head and licks the bottom of the shot glass.
- Emma and Charles have their first real conversation – that is, Emma talks, and Charles listens. They even go to her room (gasp!) to look at mementos of her days as a schoolgirl at the convent. She complains about the hired help, complains about not living in the city, and generally talks a *lot* about herself. Charles is charmed.
- On his way home, Charles mulls over the pros and cons of starting something with Emma. He begins to wonder if another marriage might be a good idea…
- Monsieur Rouault, we discover, is not averse to this idea. He loves Emma, but he's come to terms with the fact that she is simply useless on the farm. He himself isn't a big fan of farming, and really doesn't enjoy his profession. When he notices Charles's interest in Emma, he decides to give his blessing.
- After a while, Charles finally builds up the courage ask Monsieur Rouault for Emma's hand in marriage. In typical fashion, Charles can't even get the words out – fortunately, his future father-in-law figures out what's going on and says it's all cool with him. The

Madame Bovary
Shmoop Learning Guide

- marriage ball is rolling.
- Notably, we don't know what Emma thinks about any of this...
- The winter passes, and Emma busily prepares her trousseau (a fancy word for the bridal wardrobe).
- Emma reveals herself to be something of a romantic ninny; she would like to be married by torchlight in the dead of night. However, her more practical fiancé and father decide that this is probably not the best idea. A traditional wedding is planned.

Part I, Chapter Four

- It's the big day, and various friends and family members arrive in a bustle of horses, carriages, and passengers. Flaubert treats us to a rather ridiculous description of country folks; we are reminded again that this is not the sophisticated big city event that Emma longs for; rather, it is a procession of people awkwardly dressed up in their unfashionable best for a small-town wedding.
- We don't get to see the ceremony, but the wedding feast that comes afterwards is mouth-watering. The guests are treated to be huge table overflowing with roast beef, mutton, chickens, a suckling pig, many alcohols, and a dizzyingly fancy (and incredibly silly) wedding cake. The guests gorge themselves until nightfall, when they pile back into their vehicles and raucously drive back home.
- As everyone settles in for the night, a group of whiny wedding guests complain about how unsatisfactory the event was, cursing Monsieur Rouault behind his back (if you haven't already figured it out, Flaubert is highly attuned to the flaws and ironies of...well, of humanity on the whole).
- The Bovary family members are characteristically unimpressive during all of these goings-on. Charles's mother holds her tongue for once (though we can be sure that she's internally judging everything), while his father stays up partying and drinking all night with the guests. Charles himself is, as usual, fairly dull on the day of the wedding – but after the wedding *night*, he's a changed man. He's clearly very, very in love with Emma.
- The bride, on the other hand, is pretty casual about the whole thing.
- After the couple leaves to start their married life, Monsieur Rouault reflects upon his own life and his dear, departed wife. He remembers happier times and, overcome by sadness, heads home alone.
- Charles and Emma return to his house in Tostes; the neighbors show up to check out the new arrival.

Part I, Chapter Five

- Next, we get a brief tour of Charles and Emma's house. It sounds pretty decent – nothing impressive, but a nice enough home for a country doctor and his wife. There's a little garden, an office for Charles (with a bunch of unopened medical books), and generally everything a typical village housewife might need.

Madame Bovary
Shmoop Learning Guide

- Emma, however, is *not* your typical village housewife. First of all, she notices the former Madame Bovary's bridal bouquet preserved in the bedroom – this totally doesn't fly. This relic of wife #1 is relegated to exile in the attic. After this change, Emma goes on a total renovation rampage, making changes to every aspect of the little house's décor.
- Charles is in heaven. He gives in to all of Emma's whims, and buys everything she wants. He's totally head over heels in love with her, and is infatuated by her beauty. Everything is perfect, as far as he's concerned, and he can't remember ever being happier. The whole world is wrapped up in Emma.
- Emma, however, isn't sure that she's so happy. She had thought herself in love before the marriage, but now conjugal life doesn't seem so blissful. She wonders if the words she's read about in books – passion, rapture, bliss – can apply to her life.

Part I, Chapter Six

- Now that we've had a tour of the Bovary household, it's time for a tour of Emma's inner landscape. Fade out to a flashback…
- Emma is a dreamy, romantic child, and is perhaps too heavily influenced by *Paul and Virginia*, a popular and super-utopian novel about two siblings stranded on a desert island.
- At age thirteen, Emma is sent to a convent school, where she quickly falls in love with the mystical, aesthetic atmosphere of the religious life; she devotes herself to the ceremonies and artistic poses of convent life.
- We can see where this is heading. The things Emma likes best about religion aren't what you'd hope or expect – you know, stuff like *God* or *faith*. Instead, she is really into the romantic aspects of it; metaphors for the nun's relationship with God like "betrothed" and "heavenly lover" (I.6.5) really get her going.
- At the convent, Emma meets an old lady with an aristocratic background (her family was ruined by the Revolution, and she worked at the convent as a seamstress). She introduces Emma to novels – and thus to a whole new world of swoony romantic dreams. As she does her work, the girls listen to her stories and read the romance novels she carries around in her apron pocket.
- Soon enough, Emma's attentions turn from religious ecstasy to dreams of historical romance. She wishes she could live the life she read about in her books.
- Emma's mother dies while Emma is away at school; the girl is dramatically sad for a little while, but is kind of secretly pleased at herself for being so sensitive.
- The nuns worry that they've lost Emma – they'd assumed that she would join the sisterhood. She rebels against their attempts to draw her back in, and ends up leaving the convent. As Flaubert states pointedly, "no one was sorry to see her go" (I.VI.13).
- Back home, Emma enjoys playing lady of the manor and ordering the servants around for a while. However, she gets sick of it soon enough and – surprise, surprise – misses the convent. By the time Charles appears on the scene, she feels cynical and experienced (though she really hasn't *done* anything).
- She actually believes that she's in love with Charles – but we get the feeling that she would have felt the same way about any guy who happened to wander into her life at that time. Unsurprisingly, now that they're married, she's unsettled and discontented.

Madame Bovary
SHMOOP LEARNING GUIDE

Part I, Chapter Seven

- Emma wonders if these "honeymoon days" (I.7.1) are really the best days of her life. She starts to feel cheated, as though Charles has deprived her of the clichéd, romantic fantasies she cooks up. She's sure that she would be happier if only she was somewhere else…preferably with someone else…
- Emma wants to reveal these feelings of discontent to somebody, and wishes Charles could be a little more sensitive. Day by day he just grows less and less interesting to her, and she is consistently disappointed in the man she married. She believes that men should know everything and be able to do anything – Charles, however, is just an average guy.
- Emma attempts to express her turbulent feelings through drawing and music; Charles loves to watch her, and the people of the village are impressed by her accomplishments.
- Speaking of which, Emma turns out to actually be a pretty capable wife when she tries. She knows how to take care of the house and of Charles's business, and this makes the village respect the doctor and his young wife even more.
- Charles is also extremely impressed himself for having such a terrific wife. In his view, everything is just peachy keen. As far as we can tell, he's a really simple creature, with very few desires and no ambition at all. He's stingy and kind of oafish, but is generally still the same old predictable Charles – the kind of nice guy that finishes last.
- Charles's mom approves of her son's ways wholeheartedly, but she's skeptical of her daughter-in-law. She's worried that Emma wastes too much money, and every time she visits (which seems to occur pretty frequently), the two women harass each other relentlessly. This springs largely from Mom's anxieties about Charles's love for Emma – she's no longer the favorite, now that Wife #2 is in the picture.
- Charles is caught in the crossfire between the two loves of his life. He can't believe that his mother could ever be wrong, but he also can't believe that Emma ever makes any mistakes. It's a confusing time for him; mostly, he just bumbles about, which doesn't help.
- Emma decides to at least attempt to "experience love" (I.7.13). She sings songs and recites poetry to Charles, but it doesn't accomplish anything.
- That's it. Emma is certain she doesn't love Charles, and furthermore, that she's incapable of loving him. She's way, *way* bored with her life on the whole.
- One of the great constants in life is the fact that Puppies Are Awesome. Emma receives a little greyhound pup as a gift from one of Charles's patients, and for a while, the awesomeness of the puppy actually makes her feel a wee bit better. She names the dog Djali and tells her about the troubles of married life. You may not have realized it, but dog is woman's best friend, too.
- Emma is certain she could have married someone different – and better – given the chance. She wonders about her former classmates from the convent school, and is sure that they have better husbands than she does. Her former life seems painfully far away.
- Just when it seems like nothing will ever happen for Emma, an invitation arrives: she and Charles are invited to a party at the home of a local big-shot, the Marquis d'Andervilliers. The Marquis, a former patient of Charles's, was impressed by Emma's elegance.
- The chapter ends as the couple arrives at the Marquis' château.

Madame Bovary
Shmoop Learning Guide

Part I, Chapter Eight

- The château is everything Emma could have dreamt of. It's gorgeous and extravagantly beautiful. Emma is profoundly impressed by the whole thing and notices every detail.
- At dinner, Emma sees that many of the ladies take wine at dinner (putting one's glove in one's wineglass means "No thanks," and in the circles Emma grew up in, women just don't drink).
- Emma is fascinated by an old, unattractive man, the Duc de Laverdière; rumor has it that he had been Marie Antoinette's lover.
- Emma gets her first taste of champagne, pomegranates, and pineapple. Everything here seems better than it is at home. We get the feeling that she finally feels she's getting what she deserves.
- Getting dressed for the ball, Emma and Charles have a little spat. Charles wants to dance, but Emma claims it's ridiculous, saying that people will laugh at him.
- On this night, Emma looks better than ever. Charles, taken with her beauty, attempts to kiss her, but she just shoos him away.
- The ball is like one of Emma's romantic daydreams. It's filled with beautiful women in gorgeous dresses and jewels, and – to Emma's excitement – with beautiful men, too. Everything about these gorgeous guys radiates wealth, from their clear, white complexions to their well-cut clothes.
- Emma and Charles are clearly in a brand new world. Emma sees some peasants looking in through the windows, and is reminded of her former life on the farm at Les Bertaux. These new visions of luxury and beauty totally sweep her off her feet, and she begins to wonder if she ever really was a simple country girl.
- Emma witnesses a lady and gentleman exchange a secret love note.
- Hours into the ball, a second gourmet meal is served. After this, people start to leave. By 3am, it's time for the last dance, a waltz. Emma dances with a man Flaubert simply calls the Viscount, despite the fact that she doesn't really know how to waltz. She stumbles, then watches the Viscount resume the dance with another lady.
- Charles, who's been watching (but not understanding) a game of whist at the card table all night, takes Emma up to bed, complaining all the way about his tired legs.
- Emma stays up late, looking out the window and hoping to prolong her stay in this fantastical other world. Eventually she lets herself fall asleep.
- In the morning, the remaining guests eat a quick breakfast, then walk around the château's extensive grounds. Charles and Emma pack up their buggy, say their thank yous, and head back to Tostes.
- During the drive home, they encounter a party of riders on horseback. One of them, Emma thinks, is the Viscount. Shortly thereafter, Charles has to fix something on the buggy. While he's outside, he finds a green silk cigar case.
- Home again, Emma is really in a foul mood. She fires the maid, Nastasie, because dinner isn't ready on time. The word that comes to mind is "irrational."
- Charles, on the other hand, is happy to be home. He's a little sad to see Nastasie go, since she's gone through a lot with him, but doesn't want to argue with his wife.
- After dinner, Charles tries to act like an aristocratic man by smoking one of the cigars he

**Madame Bovary
Shmoop Learning Guide**

- found in the silk case. Embarrassingly, he makes himself rather ill. Emma is disgusted.
- In the following days, Emma rehashes the ball over and over again in her mind. She tries to remember everything about it.

Part I, Chapter Nine

- When Charles is out, Emma lovingly looks at the green silk cigar case and invents stories about its origins. She imagines that an adoring mistress gave it to the Viscount – she even imagines herself in the role of the mistress.
- Paris becomes a new obsession for Emma. She jealously looks at the fishmongers' carts on their way through the village, thinking about their journey to the capital city. She buys herself a map of Paris, and studies it endlessly, imagining herself there.
- In her passion for the metropolis, Emma attempts to cultivate herself by reading magazines about arts and culture. She learns all the details of fine Parisian life, and reads the novels of Honoré de Balzac and George Sand (two authors that wrote about Parisian society). In these books, she finds more and more similarities between the Viscount of her imagination and the characters.
- To Emma, everything seems possible in Paris, a city of languid, beautifully-dressed women and extravagant, thrilling men. Everything else fades around her, and Emma lives completely in the fantastical (rather ridiculous) world she constructs.
- Emma longs for luxurious boudoirs, lingering embraces, moonlit rendezvous. Instead, what she has is a number of awkward peasant servants in tattered clothes. To replace Nastasie, she hires a young girl, Félicité, who seems to be sweet but rusticated.
- With nothing else to do, Emma wanders around the house languidly, wearing a fancy dressing gown. Bored, lonely, and utterly discontented, she halfheartedly wishes both to die and to escape to Paris.
- Charles goes about his business, totally unaware of his wife's unhappiness. He's still his usual, dull self, perfectly happy and blissfully ignorant. He's just *so* pleased with everything Emma does, and by her city-like airs. She attempts to create some kind of false happiness through buying things; Charles goes along with it gamely.
- Everything looks great for Charles. His reputation as a doctor established, he generally does pretty well…that is, he doesn't kill anyone. He prescribes the same course of treatment to almost everyone: sedatives, the occasional emetic, footbath, or leeches, and on special occasions, he bleeds people or pulls teeth. He attempts to keep current with the latest medical news by subscribing to a professional journal, but it doesn't inspire him to any thrilling feats.
- Emma is fed up with all this. She wishes Charles had more ambition and intellectual oomph. She is more and more irritated by him with every passing day. Even when she straightens his clothes in an attempt to make him look more presentable, it's for her sake, not his.
- She continues to talk to Charles, however – her reasoning being that if she has to resort to talking to the dog, she might as well talk to her husband.
- Emma waits and waits, and grows more and more impatient with her unchanging life. She imagines a ship of dreams that will come and carry her away; unsurprisingly, it never does.

Madame Bovary
Shmoop Learning Guide

Every day feels the same, and she's sure that God has doomed her to a monotonous fate.
- Disgruntled, Emma gives up on all of her pastimes – she stops playing the piano, abandons her sketchbook, and ignores her embroidery. She falls into a deep depression, and feels profoundly alone. She even wishes she could chat with Félicité, but her pride stops her. It's not just Emma's life that's dull and unchanging; she observes the townspeople doing the same boring things day after day. We get the feeling that Emma's not the only person who's unenthused about provincial life.
- A wandering peddler of some kind comes around on occasions, bringing with him a hurdy-gurdy (a kind of big music box). Emma listens to the waltzes and thinks of her brush with greatness at the ball.
- Meals are the worst. Emma feels as though she can't bear it any longer, as she regards the gross-sounding meals and watches her bovine husband slowly chew his cud.
- By the springtime, Emma has given up on everything, including taking care of the house. She doesn't even make the effort to maintain her personal appearance. Her mother-in-law arrives for a visit before Easter, and is shocked by the change; she's taken aback, and can't even muster up a critical comment. Emma actually succeeds in cowing the old Madame Bovary.
- Emma starts to exhibit some kooky behavior. She goes on weird diets, has violent mood swings, and is totally unpredictable.
- At the end of February, Monsieur Rouault comes for a visit and brings a huge turkey to Emma and Charles at Tostes to celebrate the anniversary of his broken leg (nice and weird, we know). Emma spends most of the visit with him, and is surprisingly glad to see him go. He reminds her of her hick background, something for which she has a great amount of contempt.
- Actually, she's contemptuous of pretty much everyone and everything at this point, so much so that Charles is shocked by her behavior.
- All of this takes a toll on Emma's health, and Charles gets worried about her frailty. He prescribes some rather useless cures, and it makes her seem worse than ever. She demonstrates what we might call manic-depressive symptoms around this time.
- Emma complains and complains about Tostes, and Charles realizes that something about the town is making her unhappy. He ponders moving the little family elsewhere.
- Oddly, Emma starts drinking vinegar to lose weight (the nineteenth century equivalent of SlimFast?). One of Charles's old teachers diagnoses her with a so-called "nervous malady" (I.9.41), and it's decided that they'll move away.
- Charles finds a slightly larger town called Yonville-l'Abbaye that needs a doctor, and decides to move by spring if Emma stays ill.
- While preparing for the big move, Emma discovers her bridal bouquet in a drawer. While this might be a sentimental moment for some other women, she is disgusted, and throws it on the fire.
- What else could Emma and Charles *possibly* need in their complicated lives? You got it: a baby. By the time they move away in March, Emma is definitely pregnant. You can bet her mood swings aren't getting any better.

Madame Bovary
Shmoop Learning Guide

Part II, Chapter One

- Welcome to Emma and Charles's new home! Yonville-l'Abbaye, their new town, is a small step up from Tostes. It's a market town in the Neufchâtel region of France, not too far from Rouen (the closest city). The town is bordered by farmland, and it actually sounds fairly attractive. Flaubert, ever the party pooper, describes it as "characterless," and claims that it makes the worst Neufchâtel cheese in the whole district (II.I.4).
- Despite new improvements in roads and trade routes, Yonville is still really slow and old-fashioned. We can already tell that this doesn't bode well for Emma.
- The actual town is pretty simple; it has a nice house or two, a church and graveyard, some brandy distilleries and cider presses, and an inn. Most notably, it's also home to a very peculiar building: Monsieur Homais' Pharmacy. It sounds like a pretty exciting place, covered in signs advertising the pharmacist's products.
- Apparently that's all there is to see in Yonville. Our sense of dread increases. Emma is *so* not going to like this…
- The church's caretaker (also the town gravedigger), Lestiboudois, is in the practice of planting crops right up to the cemetery, a rather sketchy thing, if you ask us. The priest claims half-jokingly that he's "feeding on the dead" (II.1.13) – creepy!
- All in all, we get the picture – nothing ever changes in Yonville. It's not exactly the booming metropolis Emma dreams of.
- On the day of the Bovary's arrival, the innkeeper, Madame Lefrançois, is busy preparing everything for the coming week. She's all in a tizzy because she's got a lot of food to prepare, both for her regular boarders, and for Charles and Emma. As she's in the midst of preparations, Monsieur Homais (the pharmacist) pays her a little visit. He immediately appears to be quite an arrogant guy.
- Monsieur Homais and Madame Lefrançois have a somewhat aggressive conversation. They chat about town affairs, including a rival bar, and about the inn's boarders. Among them are an oddly dull man named Binet (the town tax collector) and some young man called Léon.
- Binet enters on cue, ready for his dinner. He seems like a normal guy, but is really, really boring. Monsieur Homais obviously isn't a huge fan.
- The town priest stops by to pick up his umbrella. He and Monsieur Homais clearly have some kind of antagonistic relationship (does this guy actually get along with anyone?), since Homais bursts out in a big anti-clerical rant after he leaves. Homais clearly regards himself as quite an intellectual. He's immoderately proud of himself.
- Finally, the Hirondelle (a kind of big, ugly, inexplicably yellow stagecoach) pulls up with the Bovarys inside. The driver, Hivert, is immediately besieged by questions from the townspeople (along with driving the coach, he runs errands for people in Rouen).
- Hivert explains the Hirondelle's tardiness: Emma's beloved greyhound, Djali, ran away and they had to stop to look for her. She was nowhere to be found. A local merchant, Monsieur Lheureux, who was along for the ride, attempts to console Emma by telling her that Djali will find her way home.

Madame Bovary
Shmoop Learning Guide

Part II, Chapter Two

- Emma, Charles, Félicité, and Monsieur Lheureux get out of the Hirondelle for the Bovarys' first glimpse of Yonville. Monsieur Homais is on hand to introduce himself.
- Emma checks out the inn. Meanwhile, a blond young man checks *her* out.
- Who is this guy, you may ask? Flaubert tells us. It turns out that this is the Monsieur Léon (Dupuis) mentioned earlier. He's a clerk who works for the notary in town. He, like Emma, is a bored young person trapped in a town full of aging, dull people.
- The dinner party, comprised of Emma, Charles, Homais, and Léon, make polite chitter chatter about their trip, and about the town. Homais goes off on a long spiel about Yonville. We realize that his primary mode of communication is probably by long spiel.
- Léon and Emma are clearly on the same wavelength – one that nobody else is on. They seem to have similar ideas and interests.
- It turns out that Léon is an amateur musician, like Emma. Monsieur Homais, with whom the young clerk lives, claims that Léon is a beautiful singer. Emma is intrigued.
- Emma and Léon have a little moment, in which he reveals that he loves German music, "the kind that makes you dream" (II.1.9) – what an Emma-like thing to say! He also tells her he's going away to Paris to study to be lawyer.
- Homais and Charles have obviously been conversing on their own. Homais attempts to include everyone in the conversation; Emma and Léon aren't interested, and soon get caught up in their private conversation again.
- Like Emma, Léon is a big reader, and it seems like they have pretty similar thoughts about literature, as well.
- Homais tries to break into their conversation again, offering the use of his personal library to Emma.
- Emma and Léon are sitting so close that he has his feet on one of the rungs of her chair.
- After dinner, the guests all go their separate ways. Emma and Charles go into their new house for the first time. It doesn't sound too thrilling. We are unsurprised.
- Emma philosophically muses that, since her life so far hasn't been too hot, it has to get better.

Part II, Chapter Three

- The next morning, Emma sees Léon through her bedroom window; they bow to each other.
- Léon, hopeful that the Bovarys will turn up for dinner at the inn again, can't wait for six o'clock. However, dinnertime rolls around, and Emma is nowhere to be found. He's deeply disappointed.
- Apparently, Léon isn't exactly a lady's man. His conversation with Emma the previous night was the most intimate situation he's ever been in with a "lady." Everyone in the town likes him for his many fine qualities, but he felt a different kind of connection with Emma.
- Homais turns out to be a very, *very* attentive neighbor. He gives Emma all kinds of assistance with the house, and is oh-so-friendly. However, he's not exactly Ned Flanders. It seems that his kindly guy-next-door act is a front; he'd been accused previously of

Madame Bovary
Shmoop Learning Guide

- illegally practicing medicine without any certification, and was threatened with legal action. A lot of townspeople, including the mayor, are out to get him, so he's careful to keep Charles on his side.
- Speaking of Charles, the poor guy isn't so happy. He doesn't have any patients yet, and spends most of his time hanging about the house. He's worried about money – the move from Tostes was expensive, and all the money that Emma brought with her to the marriage is gone.
- The only thing that cheers Charles up is the thought of Emma's pregnancy. He feels that his whole life is complete now that a baby is on the horizon.
- Emma, on the other hand, traversed a whole range of emotions, from astonished to bitter, before settling on indifferent. She decides that if she must have a baby, it should be a boy, so it can have the power to escape the rules that govern women.
- Instead, it's a girl.
- Emma passes out, presumably from disappointment, as well as the rigors of childbirth. Madame Homais and Madame Lefrançois rush in to see how things are going. Everyone is excited except Emma.
- Emma can't even think up a name for the poor kid. She has all kinds of romantic ideas about what she'd like to call the daughter (um, *Galsuinde*? Seriously?). Homais has all kinds of crazy ideas, naturally, having named his children all kinds of crazy things. Emma eventually settles haphazardly on "Berthe."
- Little Berthe is baptized. Her godfather is Homais, since Emma's dad couldn't make it for the birth, and her godmother is old Madame Bovary, who's visiting with her husband.
- Charles's father gets along pretty well with Emma, who's interested in his stories of travel in the army. Charles's mom is worried that her husband will be a bad influence upon Emma, and they peace out pretty quickly.
- One day, as Emma is going to visit the baby (who's staying with Madame Rollet, a wetnurse in another part of town), she runs into Léon. She invites him to come with her, which causes quite the scandal among the gossips of the town.
- The wetnurse lives in an unsavory little cottage. Léon is thrown off by the image before him, of the beautiful lady in a fancy dress surrounded by squalor. The baby makes a spectacular entrance by promptly spitting up on Emma. The visitors head out.
- As they're leaving, Madame Rollet comes up and wheedles the promise of some brandy out of Emma.
- Emma and Léon head back to Yonville. They obviously have an intense connection already.
- When they get back to town, Emma heads home, while Léon keeps wandering, pondering his boredom and the dullness of the other people he knows in town. He has quite the crush on our young Madame Bovary.

Part II, Chapter Four

- Once the winter arrives, Emma moves into the parlor from her room. She sits and people-watches all day.
- Twice a day, she sees Léon go back and forth to and from his office.

Madame Bovary
Shmoop Learning Guide

- Monsieur Homais continues to be an attentive neighbor; he stops by every day around dinner time to discuss the daily news with Charles and to give Emma household tips.
- After this evening chat, Justin (Homais' cousin/apprentice/servant boy) comes in to fetch his master. Homais pokes fun at the boy for having a crush on Félicité.
- The pharmacist also scolds Justin for eavesdropping all the time.
- On Sundays, the Homais household entertains the few townspeople Monsieur Homais hasn't alienated. Léon and the Bovarys always come.
- On these occasions, Léon is always by Emma's side, talking to her, coaching her at card games, and looking at magazines with her.
- Something is obviously going on between Emma and Léon. Charles, unsuspecting as ever, has no idea. At this point, Emma herself doesn't fully realize it.
- Léon is careful to include Charles in his thoughts, as to avoid suspicions. He gives the officier de santé a splendid phrenological head model for his birthday (a kind of bizarro medical fad of the nineteenth century – supposedly different head shapes have different meanings).
- Léon is always willing to get things for Emma, from the latest books to a bushel of cacti.
- Emma and Léon each have little gardens outside their windows, from which they look at each other while tending the plants.
- To show her gratitude, Emma has a gorgeous velvet bedspread sent over to Léon…it seems like something of an extravagant present. Everyone else is sure that the pair are lovers.
- Léon idiotically reinforces this idea by talking about Emma 24/7. Even poor Binet gets so sick of him that he snaps at the boy one day.
- Ah, l'amour! Léon is tortured by his love for Emma, and tries to figure out how to possibly tell her. He can't bring himself to do it.
- Emma, on the other hand, doesn't get all worked up; she doesn't even try and see if she is or isn't in love with him. Flaubert ominously ends the chapter, though, with the suggestion that one day she'll crack and her love will be out of control.

Part II, Chapter Five

- The usual quartet is out on an odd and incredibly boring field trip. They're visiting a new spinning mill just outside town, along with two of Homais' unfortunately named children, Athalie and Napoléon.
- The main attraction is generally unattractive.
- Homais, as usual, chats up a storm. Everyone else is somewhat pensive. Emma reflects suddenly upon how irritating Charles is, even when he's doing nothing.
- Léon, on the other hand, looks particularly lovely to her. She begins to realize that something is happening between them.
- Napoléon ruins the moment by generally being bratty. He's painted his shoes white with a pile of lime that's lying around the mill. Charles and Justin attempt to get rid of it.
- That evening, Emma thinks about the day – and about Léon. She can't stop envisioning his face, his mannerisms, the sound of his voice. Finally, an epiphany: Léon loves her!
- Once she admits this to herself, Emma goes into full-out dramatic Love Overdrive. She

Madame Bovary
Shmoop Learning Guide

- laments fate, lolls around the house swooning left and right, and drifts about in a blissful haze. Generally, she does everything she's read about in books.
- The next day, Monsieur Lheureux, the dry-goods merchant (he sells things like fabric and pretty much any household item) stops by for a visit. He is quite clever and sounds, from Flaubert's description, like a pretty shady character. Nobody knows what he was up to before he came to Yonville.
- The merchant knows exactly what buttons to press with Emma. He talks up her elegance and refinement, then offers her a selection of dainty items to choose from. She sticks by her guns and says she doesn't need anything, but the seed has been planted – Emma, naturally, wants pretty things.
- Lheureux also slyly tells Emma that if she needs money, she can always borrow it from him…which doesn't sound like such a great idea, if you ask us.
- Emma congratulates herself on being so frugal, but she still can't stop thinking of Monsieur Lheureux's pretty wares.
- Léon shows up, nervous and on edge. He wants to say something to her about his feelings, but chickens out yet again. Awkwardness ensues.
- In the wake of the realization that she and Léon are in love, Emma attempts briefly to reform herself – she goes all serious and tries to clean up her act.
- Emma's good girl façade fools everyone, even Léon. He begins to wonder how he'd even hoped to get close to her. In his mind, she becomes even more spectacular and flawless.
- Everyone admires Emma for her elegance and character. Now that she's playing the good housewife, she floats along easily in Yonville society. However, on the inside, she conceals passionate feelings. We're talking *serious* angst, here. When she's alone, she can only think of Léon – actually, these fantasies are more enjoyable than his presence, which leaves her unsatisfied.
- Emma wishes Léon would notice that she's in love with him, but she's either too lazy or too scared to make anything happen herself. She consoles herself by striking dramatic poses in the mirror and prides herself on her "virtue."
- All of Emma's secret troubles build up to the boiling point, and she strikes out, complaining about the littlest things, like a door left open or a dish she doesn't enjoy.
- She is also incredibly irritated by Charles's dopey lack of awareness; he's still sure that he's making her perfectly happy. She feels underappreciated, and makes Charles the focus of all her aggression.
- Emma's depression returns from time to time. Félicité tries to comfort her, telling her that she once knew another girl who suffered from a similar problem – it was cured by marriage. Unfortunately for Emma, her sadness was brought on by her marriage to Charles.

Part II, Chapter Six

- Poor Emma. It's springtime, and she finally attempts to do *something* to change her life. Remembering how much she loved the convent school, she goes to church to talk to Father Bournisien.
- She finds the priest much preoccupied by the schoolboys he's in charge of. He's

Madame Bovary
Shmoop Learning Guide

- something of an irritable and unpleasant man.
- Emma flat-out tells the priest that she's suffering. He assumes that her suffering is physical, and asks if Charles has prescribed anything for it. When Emma attempts to explain her situation, he gets distracted by the boys again, and breaks off the conversation to yell at them.
- This is hopeless. The priest obviously has nothing to offer Emma – they talk for a while longer, their conversation punctuated by the children. Father Bournisien eventually just dismisses Emma, telling her to go home and have a cup of tea. She leaves, disgruntled.
- When she gets home, the stillness of the house seems to mock her. Berthe tries to come over and hug her mother. Emma (who, if you hadn't guessed, is a *terrible mother*), angrily pushes the little girl away. Pushing a baby? Come on, Emma. This is a new low.
- Poor Berthe falls and hits her head on the dresser. She starts to bleed, and Emma freaks out. She feels terrible.
- Charles comes home, and Emma tells him that the baby fell over while she was playing. He takes care of the injury and tells Emma not to worry. Emma feels bad for a while, but her anxiety eventually wears off. She looks at Berthe dispassionately, thinking about how ugly the child is.
- Charles, in the meanwhile, has been visiting the Homais family. Mr. and Mrs. Homais. try to cheer him up in a truly warped way, by talking about the various dangers that children face in their everyday lives. The Homais kids live in a totally child-safe household without sharp knives and with bars on the windows.
- Léon is also around. Charles pulls him aside – the clerk worries that the doctor suspects his feelings for Emma.
- Luckily for Léon, Charles is still the same old well-intentioned buffoon he always was. He actually wants Léon to go into Rouen for him and make some inquiries about getting a portrait of Charles made.
- It turns out that Léon goes into the city every week – nobody knows why. Homais suspects that the young man has a secret lover there (wrong!). Nobody can figure out what Léon's deal is.
- Madame Lefrançois notices that he's started leaving food on his plate at dinner. Binet suggests that Léon should take up carpentry to improve his disposition (a rather odd choice).
- Léon's boredom with Yonville and angst about his love for Emma are at a breaking point. However, he's also afraid of moving away. In the end, though, he decides to leave right away for Paris, to start his studies in the big city.
- Soon enough it's time to go. The Homais give Léon a tearful seeing-off, but before he leaves, he goes to bid Charles and Emma farewell.
- Charles isn't at home, so he and Emma have a tense parting moment. He kisses baby Berthe goodbye, then he and Emma are left alone. They shake hands awkwardly – the tension is palpable.
- Léon leaves Yonville, accompanied by the notary, Monsieur Guillaumin.
- After he's gone, Emma mopes around, wondering where he is. Monsieur Homais comes over to visit as usual, and they discuss Léon's fate in Paris.
- Homais and Charles are worried that Léon will be corrupted by the city, or else catch some horrible disease. Emma is distressed.
- Soon enough, though, Homais acts as though nothing has happened. He heads back home merrily.

Part II, Chapter Seven

- Emma sinks back into depression. Now that Léon is gone, she has nothing but her romantic fantasies left. It's just like it was after the ball at La Vaubyessard – nothing seems good enough for her.
- Léon becomes the center of Emma's fantasy life – not the *real* Léon, mind you, but her own construction of him. Now that he's gone, she curses herself for never giving into her love and…how shall we put this delicately…en*ffering* herself to him.
- The memory of Léon becomes the center of Emma's life; Flaubert compares this memory to a campfire burning in the middle of a desolate, snow-covered plain. Emma clings to it desperately for a while, but soon enough it dies down.
- Eventually, the flame of Emma's love for Léon dies completely, and she's left in the dark. Her depression is again as intense as it was in Tostes. Emma melodramatically feels that her life will *never* be better now that she's experienced something she thinks is real grief.
- This time around, Emma attempts to console herself with material things. She goes on a shopping spree, purchasing a special prie-dieu (a kind of prayer bench), new clothes, and a variety of other pricey things. She also half-heartedly picks up some new hobbies, like learning Italian and reading "serious" books instead of novels, but quickly abandons them. She also acts with an astounding unpredictability – one day she even downs a whole glass of brandy, much to Charles's dismay.
- Emma is flighty and unpredictable, but she never seems to swing over to "happy." Her looks reflect her inner unhappiness, and she starts to complain about aging.
- Her health is on the decline on the whole – one day she even spits up some blood. Charles is understandably worried, but Emma waves him off. She seems not to care whether she lives or dies.
- Charles cares, though. This incident reduces him to tears, and the only thing he can think to do is write to his mother.
- The elder Madame Bovary suggests rather vehemently that it's Emma's novels and lack of religion that make her ill – so Charles decides to keep Emma from reading them. He's afraid to tell this to Emma himself, so his mother comes to take care of the matter. She cancels Emma's library card herself.
- Emma and her mother-in-law are *not* happy to see each other – Madame Bovary Senior leaves after three weeks of uncomfortable silence.
- Mama Bovary leaves on a market-day and, after she's gone, Emma hangs out her window, watching the merchants assembled sell their wares. In the crowd, she notices a real live gentleman in a fancy velvet coat. Shockingly, he's headed towards the Bovary house.
- The gentleman asks Justin and Félicité if Charles is available – apparently his servant isn't feeling well and wants to be bled.
- Charles gets Justin to help with the operation by holding a basin to catch the blood. The sight of blood is too much for both the servant and for Justin – both of them pass out cold. Emma has to come and assist with the remainder of the business.
- Emma is undisturbed by the blood. She competently helps Charles and attempts to revive Justin. As she helps her husband, she looks particularly beautiful, even amidst all the

Madame Bovary
Shmoop Learning Guide

- mess.
- Homais comes over, just as all of this is happening. He yells at Justin for hanging about the Bovary household instead of working in the pharmacy where he belongs; the boy heads back home.
- The remaining party briefly discusses fainting – Emma has never done it. Monsieur Boulanger comments that it's very rare that a lady should have such a strong constitution, but notes that some men are also really easily disturbed by blood.
- Monsieur Boulanger sends his servant back home, but lingers to pay…and get a better look at Emma.
- He's shocked by how beautiful and graceful Emma is, and can't believe that she's married to Charles. We get the idea that Rodolphe Boulanger is bad, bad news. He's handsome, brutish, and intelligent – a dangerous combination. Furthermore, he's a real womanizer. Emma is out of her league with this guy.
- Rodolphe decides to seduce Emma. He's incredibly arrogant about it – he thinks he has her all figured out. Unfortunately, he's right.

Part II, Chapter Eight

- It's a big day for little Yonville – the town fair. Everyone in the town is up early to set up for it. Binet, who doubles as the captain of the fire brigade, is all gussied up. The whole town is looking its best.
- The only person who's not too thrilled about all of this is Madame Lefrançois. Homais stops to chat with her, and she cheers up a little when she finds out that he's on the fair advisory committee (he got there through a dubious claim that his knowledge of chemistry gives him advanced knowledge of farming).
- Homais keeps talking, but his audience is not listening. We follow Madame Lefrançois' gaze and see what has put her in such a foul mood – the town's other tavern, her rival, is full of singing people. These good days won't last too long, though; she tells Homais that she heard that Tellier, the barkeep, was in such great debt to Monsieur Lheureux that the tavern was going to be shut down the following week.
- From the perspective of these gossiping neighbors, we see Emma and Rodolphe a little ways off, talking to Monsieur Lheureux. Rodolphe is obviously planning on making his move already – unlike Léon, he's a pretty smooth operator.
- Homais goes over to say hello, but Rodolphe manages to avoid him. He regards Emma as they walk along – he's pleased with what he sees.
- Monsieur Lheureux attempts to follow them and maintain their conversation, but they get rid of him quickly. Rodolphe immediately launches his attack and starts flirting openly with Emma once they're alone.
- The townspeople are assembled for various agricultural competitions. Rodolphe is supposed to participate in the judging, but he has other things on his mind. He turns all his attention to Emma, who responds eagerly to him.
- He knows exactly what buttons to push – they talk about the frustrations of provincial life, the loneliness of existence…basically, all of Emma's favorite subjects.
- Their conversation is interrupted by the entrance of the fire brigade and the start of the

Madame Bovary
Shmoop Learning Guide

- awards ceremony. A government official, Monsieur Lieuvain, arrives to dole out the prizes; he gives a long, long, *loooong* speech about the government, the country.
- While this is going on, Emma and Rodolphe continue their intimate conversation. Rodolphe claims that the only true duty is to enjoy what's beautiful about life, and reject the conventions of society.
- Emma feebly tries to argue that society's moral standards are important, but Rodolphe shoots her down promptly. He's the clear winner here; Emma is toast.
- Monsieur Lieuvain, in the meanwhile, just keeps talking and talking. He's full of governmental rhetoric, but he's basically not talking about anything. Despite this fact, the whole town (except for Emma and Rodolphe) is enraptured by him.
- Rodolphe quickly wins Emma over. All of her feelings about Léon, the Viscount at the ball, and her loneliness come rushing back, and re-focus on Rodolphe. She's smitten.
- Finally, Monsieur Lieuvain wraps up his speech. Another speech begins, and Rodolphe continues to woo Emma all the while.
- Agricultural prizes are given for things as diverse as pigs, liquid manure (gross), and drainage. Simultaneously (in an inspired moment of truly ridiculous juxtaposition), Rodolphe declares his love for Emma.
- The prizes, and the wooing, conclude with the awarding of a prize for long service, which is awarded to a confused little old woman. Flaubert describes this woman, Catherine Leroux, with rather excruciating detail; she's obviously been broken down by years of hard work. She says that she will give her prize money to the priest, which offends Homais.
- Following this ludicrous ceremony, a big feast begins. The townspeople, in a frenzy of communal gluttony, all stuff themselves.
- Rodolphe isn't interested in the food – he's thinking of Emma and of the pleasure he'll get from her in the future. Emma is off with Charles and the Homais family.
- The grand finale of the festival is a display of fireworks – unfortunately, they're too damp, and they barely go off. The evening ends rather anti-climactically, and everyone drifts back home.
- Homais proceeds to write an enthusiastic, over-the-top article about the fiesta, and publish it in a Rouen paper.

Part II, Chapter Nine

- Six weeks have passed since the fair. Rodolphe hasn't seen Emma again; at first, he just didn't want to show up to see her right away, and decided to go on a hunting trip. However, this trip lasted a lot longer than he'd planned and, now that he's back, he's worried that he missed his window of opportunity.
- He decides to give it a shot anyway and visit Emma, hoping that absence has indeed made the heart grow fonder.
- Again, he's right. He can immediately tell that Emma's still totally into him. He plays his absence up melodramatically, claiming that he had to tear himself away from her. Rodolphe is a total drama king (and *liar*), and he theatrically wins Emma over with highfalutin' words and extravagant declarations of passion.
- Emma is totally swept off her feet by Rodolphe's calculated attack. She allows herself to

Madame Bovary
Shmoop Learning Guide

bask in the glow of his romantic words. However, as he continues to ham it up, they hear Charles arrive at the house. The two lovers immediately switch back into polite neighbor mode.
- Rodolphe, ever the resourceful one, asks Charles if it might do Emma some good to take up horseback riding to improve her health. Of course, he will accompany her himself.
- Charles thinks this is a splendid idea, and he and Rodolphe make all the arrangements. Emma, in a contrary mood, resists – however, Charles convinces her by saying that she can order a new riding outfit.
- The next day, Rodolphe shows up promptly at noon on horseback, with a second horse in tow for Emma. After a brief warning about safety from Monsieur Homais, they're off.
- The pair ride off into the countryside. They get a good view of the village from up higher – to Emma, Yonville has never looked so small and miserable.
- They venture deeper and deeper into the forest. They dismount and Rodolphe ties up the horses so they can walk into the woods unhampered. As they go, he keeps his eyes on the sliver of white stocking that show between her skirt and boots – to him, it seems like naked skin.
- Rodolphe and Emma reach a clearing and, once they're settled down, he starts to woo her once more…this time more seriously.
- Emma puts up some resistance – but not too much. She gives in to his advances and, as Flaubert says, "abandons" herself to him. We all know what that means.
- After the deed is done, Rodolphe and Emma head back to Yonville slowly. Everything seems different to her now.
- Rodolphe is legitimately charmed by her – after all, she's quite lovely.
- Emma feels as though everyone is looking at her as they ride through town.
- At dinner, Charles tells her that he's purchased a horse of her very own. Little does he know what's really going on…
- Emma escapes from dinner early and goes upstairs to think over her situation in privacy. She even thinks she looks different – and she feels as though her real life is finally starting.
- From the next day on, Emma and Rodolphe are committed to each other (at least, she's committed to him, and believes him when he says loves her).
- They do the stereotypical things people having affairs do – exchange notes, have secret rendezvous, etc.
- Emma is blissfully happy. She even runs out in the early morning (after Charles has left on an early call) and races over to La Huchette to see her lover.
- After this risky business goes on for a while, Rodolphe protests that she's getting too careless. Is he really concerned, or can it be that he's getting sick of her? Hmm…

Part II, Chapter Ten

- This warning from Rodolphe begins to worry Emma – and one day, she encounters Binet illegally duck hunting. He has his own worries, since he's breaking the law, but Emma begins to fear that he will tell everyone he saw her gadding about in the wee hours of the morning.
- She stresses out about this all day. In the evening, Charles insists that they go get

Madame Bovary
Shmoop Learning Guide

- something to perk herself up from Monsieur Homais.
- While they're at the pharmacist's, they happen to run into Binet, who makes a knowing comment about the humid weather, referencing their encounter that morning in the mist.
- This alarms Emma. She's relieved when Binet leaves.
- The Binet incident makes Emma and Rodolphe rethink their meeting strategy. They decide that Rodolphe will look for a safe place to meet. In the meanwhile, they meet late at night in the back garden of the Bovarys' house, after Charles has gone to sleep (doesn't that seem a little risky, too?).
- Léon is all but forgotten by this time.
- One night, Emma hears someone coming, and worries that it's Charles. She asks Rodolphe if he has pistols with which to defend himself against her husband. Rodolphe finds this concern absurd and in poor taste. In fact, he's beginning to find many of Emma's demands and goings-on rather vulgar.
- Emma's ridiculously romantic fantasies run wild with Rodolphe. She makes him exchange little tokens of love and locks of hair, and demands that they get a real wedding ring as a symbol of their devotion.
- All of this irritates Rodolphe, but he's still drawn to her – he can't believe how pretty and charming she can be. However, he stops putting forth as much effort soon enough, and their affair loses its initial quality of excitement and oomph.
- By the time spring rolls around, the affair has cooled to a markedly un-steamy temperature. The two of them are like a married couple.
- Monsieur Rouault sends his customary anniversary turkey to celebrate the healing of his broken leg. With it comes a letter – reading it reminds Emma of the days of her childhood in the country. Looking back, those days seem idyllic to her now. She wonders what has made her adult life so difficult.
- For a brief moment, looking at her innocent young daughter, Emma actually loves little Berthe.
- Rodolphe is definitely sick of Emma by now. They treat each other indifferently – Emma in an attempt to win him back and Rodolphe because he genuinely feels like their affair is over.
- Rejected and dejected, Emma repents for her adulterous actions – she even goes so far as to wish she could love Charles. In addition, Homais happens to give Charles the opportunity to become a more interesting man at this fortuitous time...

Part II, Chapter Eleven

- It turns out that Homais is all excited about some article on curing clubfeet. He's convinced that Charles should attempt to fix the clubfoot of Hippolyte, a servant at Madame Lefrançois's inn.
- Emma is easily convinced. She hopes that the operation will earn Charles some respect and extra cash. This helps a *lot* with her resolution to stay with him.
- Charles, despite his profound lack of medical talent, agrees to do it. He prepares for the operation by reading and attempting to understand it, while Homais works on getting Hippolyte himself to agree.

Madame Bovary
Shmoop Learning Guide

- Hippolyte gives in to the pharmacist's goading (and that of the rest of the town, who all feel involved in this process), and accepts the operation.
- Charles, in the meanwhile, is having a heck of a time figuring out how to fix Hippolyte's disfigured leg. He's clearly confused and concerned, but goes ahead gamely anyway. He ends up cutting poor Hippolyte's Achilles tendon, thinking that it's the right thing to do. Ugh, just thinking of it gives us the chills.
- After the operation, which appears at first to be a success, Emma actually voluntarily embraces Charles. The two of them are happier together than we've ever seen them. She is finally able to muster up a little bit of affection for poor Charles, who she now views as an up-and-coming surgeon in the making.
- Homais busily writes up the operation for the Rouen paper, claiming that it's a complete success.
- However, this honeymoon period doesn't last. Five days after the operation, Madame Lefrançois bursts in, claiming that Hippolyte is dying. Charles and Homais rush off to see what's wrong.
- Gaah! What *isn't* wrong would be a better question. Hippolyte's foot is a disgusting mass of infection, trapped within the bizarre torture device Charles strapped it into. Ignoring Hippolyte's claims of incredible pain, they put him back in the apparatus.
- Three days later, though, the infection is way, way worse – it's so disgusting we don't even want to tell you about it here. Seriously. GROSS.
- Everyone tries to make Hippolyte feel better, except for the peasants who come to the inn to play billiards. They just make him feel *worse*, and tell him that he smells bad.
- Actually, that's not just a taunt – it's true. The gangrenous leg reeks up a storm. Hippolyte is in total despair, but Charles, who has no clue how to fix it, just tells him to eat more lightly (*what?*).
- To make matters even worse, Father Bournisien comes over to harass the crippled man about his lack of religion. We're sure it didn't exactly make Hippolyte feel any better.
- Finally, Madame Lefrançois, worried about the lack of improvement, send for Monsieur Canivet, a real M.D. from Neufchâtel.
- Canivet, who is, unlike Charles, an actual *doctor*, laughs contemptuously when he sees Hippolyte's condition, and says what everyone should have known by now – the leg must be amputated. He complains to Homais about practitioners (like Charles) who make use of ridiculous procedures without a thought about the patients…or victims, rather.
- Homais feels bad, but chooses not to defend Charles – after all, Monsieur Canivet is an important man.
- The amputation is a big event for the village. Everyone is quite excited, except, presumably, for Hippolyte. Poor guy.
- Canivet struts into the town, confident in his own abilities. He derides *officiers de santé* like Charles, claiming that they ruin the reputation of doctors everywhere.
- Speaking of our old friend, Charles stays at home, miserable, embarrassed, and guilty for the part he's played in Hippolyte's disaster.
- Emma sits by him, humiliated and angry. She's mad at herself for even hoping that Charles could be anything but mediocre.
- This is the last straw for Emma. She can't believe she ever felt bad for cheating on Charles.
- The angry tension of the Bovary household is broken by a horrifying shriek that echoes through the village. The amputation is underway.

Madame Bovary
Shmoop Learning Guide

- Charles and Emma stare at each other through the sounds of Hippolyte's screams – and to Emma, everything about her husband disgusts her. Her feelings for Rodolphe come rushing back, and it's as though Charles is permanently alienated from her life from this point on.
- The operation is apparently over – they see Canivet and Homais leave the inn and return to the pharmacy.
- Despairing, Charles asks Emma to kiss him. She refuses him violently, and flees the room.
- Charles has no clue what's going on.
- That night, Emma and Rodolphe are reunited in the garden – they kiss passionately, their affair back in full bloom.

Part II, Chapter Twelve

- Emma and Rodolphe's relationship is passionate again. Sometimes Emma misses Rodolphe so badly that she sends Justin to fetch him in the middle of the day.
- On one such day, she suggests that the two of them run off and live somewhere else. Rodolphe doesn't understand why she's so serious over something as trivial as a love affair.
- Emma really *is* serious, though. The more she loves Rodolphe, the more she hates Charles – in comparison to her lover, her husband seems impossibly dull, crude, and generally icky.
- Emma's vanity really emerges here; to keep herself looking good for Rodolphe, she spends all her time thinking about her appearance and making her room ready for his visits.
- Félicité is busy all day washing lingerie for Emma. While she does the laundry, she chats to Justin, who's always hanging around. He's fascinated by the assortment of mysterious feminine garments.
- Emma's spending is clearly getting out of control. Her closets are full of shoes, which she frequently throws away and replaces. Charles doesn't make a peep about any of this.
- He also doesn't complain about the purchase of a beautiful, super-fancy prosthetic leg that Emma insists they get for Hippolyte. He's awed by the glory of this leg, and they get him plainer one for everyday wear. Hippolyte quickly goes back to work, and Charles feels guilty every time he hears the stableboy tap-tapping his ways along the street on his false leg.
- Monsieur Lheureux is Emma's new constant companion. He talks to her endlessly about the fads in Paris, and she gives in, ordering item after item. For a while, she feels safe like this – he never asks for money.
- One day, however, after Emma purchases a beautiful riding crop for Rodolphe, Lheureux suddenly shows up with a giant bill. Emma's not sure what to do – she doesn't have any money. In fact, there's no money in the whole house. She manages to put him off for a little while, but the merchant soon loses patience.
- Desperately, Emma tells him to take back the things she's bought for him. Craftily, he tells her that he only really needs the riding crop back – and he offers to ask Charles to return it. Based on her panicked reaction, he figures out the truth: she's having an affair.

Madame Bovary
Shmoop Learning Guide

- Fortunately, a big payment comes in just in time from one of Charles's patients. When Lheureux returns for his money, ready to strike some kind of devilish deal, he's shocked to see Emma offer him payment in full.
- Unfortunately, this means that the household is short on money. Emma puts this little fact out of her mind for the time being.
- Rodolphe continues to receive extravagant gifts from his mistress, which is actually really ridiculous, since *he's* the wealthy one. In addition to the riding crop, she gives him a ring, a scarf, and an embroidered cigar case like the one Charles found on the road. Rodolphe is embarrassed by the lavish presents, but accepts them anyway.
- Emma keeps making her same old foolishly romantic demands – and again, Rodolphe starts to get a little sick of it. They fight and make up over and over again; Emma lavishes praise on him, and pledges her unending devotion.
- Rodolphe, who's much more of a cynic than she is, gets fed up her melodramatic declarations.
- Rodolphe starts to cultivate new pleasures in his relationship with Emma – he seems to enjoy corrupting her and forcing her to be compliant to him. She wallows in her infatuation for him, giving in to his desires.
- Emma kind of loses it under Rodolphe's influence. She stops caring about what people think, and starts acting like what one might call a "loose woman," to use a rather outdated phrase. She starts smoking in public and wearing daringly "mannish" clothes.
- The worst of it comes when Charles's mother visits. The two women, whose relationship is already in the dumps, get into a huge fight over Félicité, of all people. Old Madame Bovary discovered Félicité with a man (gasp!) in the house in the dead of night, and accuses Emma of being immoral. Emma takes this as a class issue, claiming that her mother-in-law is just an unsophisticated, narrow-minded peasant. She tells the older woman to get out of the house.
- Poor Charles is caught in the crossfire between the two domineering women in his life once more. He helplessly tries to make things better.
- Emma gives in and apologizes to her mother-in-law – but she certainly doesn't mean it.
- She puts up an emergency signal for Rodolphe; he comes to see what's the matter, and she launches into the whole story and begs him to take her away. He doesn't exactly say yes or no.
- For the next few days, Emma acts like a new woman. She's completely docile, and even asks her mother-in-law for a recipe. Is it possible that this new behavior is for the benefit of Charles and his mom, or that it's to convince herself more fully of the repressive demands of her everyday life? No – the truth is that she's so swept up in the fantasy of running away with Rodolphe that she simply doesn't even notice anything around her.
- Emma keeps bringing up the idea of escape with Rodolphe, imagining scene after scene of their flight from Yonville.
- Emma is more beautiful than ever. Poor Charles is even more in love with her than ever.
- Charles indulges for the first time in his own flights of fancy. His dreams are centered around Emma and Berthe. He imagines an impossible future in which everyone lives happily ever after; he envisions Berthe growing as beautiful as her mother, and can almost see the two of them together, almost like sisters rather than mother and daughter.
- In the meanwhile, on the other side of the bed, Emma sees herself escaping with Rodolphe, fleeing to a new country full of fantastical, almost mythological landscapes. She doesn't imagine anything specific. In fact, her vision of the future seems almost as

Madame Bovary
Shmoop Learning Guide

consistent as her monotonous present, with one significant difference: in this future, she'll be blissfully happy.
- In preparation for her supposed elopement with Rodolphe, Emma orders a long cloak and traveling trunk from Monsieur Lheureux. He figures she's had a fight with Charles.
- Emma gives her watch to Lheureux to sell in exchange for these goods.
- Rodolphe and Emma actually set a date – they will leave the next month. She plans to make like she's going to Rouen to do some shopping, but will instead meet Rodolphe, who will have made all the travel arrangements for them to flee to Italy. Everything looks like it's actually falling into place.
- There's no mention of what will happen to little Berthe – Rodolphe hopes that Emma will just forget about her.
- Weeks pass – Rodolphe delays the trip for various reasons. All of August passes, and they decide that they will absolutely, positively leave on Monday, September 4.
- The Saturday before the trip, Rodolphe stops by. He's looking sad and particularly tender. They swear that they love each other once more.
- Rodolphe suggests that there's still time to change her mind, but Emma is sure: she is ready to leave Yonville behind.
- Rodolphe takes his leave of Emma. On his way home, he stops, filled with emotion. We discover – surprise, surprise – that he intends to desert her. He's tempted to go through with the plan – but no, he won't. Rodolphe is no fool, and he doesn't intend to become one.

Part II, Chapter Thirteen

- His mind made up, Rodolphe returns home to La Huchette and sits down to write a farewell letter to Emma.
- He sifts through the various tokens of love affairs past that he's accumulated through many years of being a ladies' man. All of the women he's had in the past blur together in his mind – now Emma is just one of them.
- Rodolphe gets down to business. He writes a truly melodramatic, ostentatiously noble letter to Emma, telling her that he can't allow himself to ruin her life, blah blah blah. Suddenly the "fate" that supposedly brought them together before is now responsible for tearing them apart.
- To avoid having to face her again, he writes that he's going on a long trip.
- The letter finished, Rodolphe is quite proud of himself. He even puts some false tearstains on the paper. This guy is just too much.
- The next day, Rodolphe wakes up late, and has Girard, one of his servants, take the letter to Emma, concealed in the bottom of a basket of apricots.
- Upon receiving basket, Emma is overcome with emotion – she finds the letter, immediately understands what its purpose is, and rushes to her room to read it.
- Charles is there, so she flees madly, running to the attic. There, she forces herself to finish the horrible letter. Her feelings are all over the place – she feels desperately as though she might as well hurl herself out the window onto the pavement below.
- Fortunately, Charles calls her from downstairs. She returns to herself, shocked that she

Madame Bovary
Shmoop Learning Guide

- narrowly avoided death.
- It's dinnertime. Félicité comes to fetch her mistress; Emma is forced to go downstairs and go through with the farce of eating. It's torture.
- To make matters worse, Charles even brings up Rodolphe, mentioning that he'd heard from Girard that the gentleman is going on a trip.
- *Then*, just when Emma doesn't think that things can possibly be more horrible, Félicité brings in the basket of apricots. Charles eats one, and tries to force Emma to, as well.
- This is too much to handle – Emma almost swoons. Charles tries to calm her, but then she sees Rodolphe's carriage pass by the window. She passes out.
- Monsieur Homais runs over when he hears chaos break out in the Bovary house. He brings some vinegar back to revive the unconscious woman.
- Emma comes back from her faint briefly – Charles, freaking out, tries to get her to hold Berthe. Emma promptly passes out again.
- Charles puts Emma to bed. He and Homais try and determine what could have possibly brought on this attack. Homais puts it down to the scent of the apricots.
- Emma stays sick for a really long time. Charles stays by her side for forty-three days in a row – like we said, a *really* long time.
- He calls in backup; Dr. Canivet is called, as well as Charles's old teacher, Dr. Larivière.
- Emma doesn't say anything or give any indication of what's causing all of this.
- By the middle of October, Emma feels well enough to sit up in bed – she starts to eat a little bit, and even gets out of bed for a few hours of the day. She recovers slowly, then relapses.
- Charles worries that she may have cancer.
- To make it even worse, there's no money.

Part II, Chapter Fourteen

- You have to feel bad for Charles. Life is not being particularly kind to him.
- First of all, he has to pay all kinds of bills, he owes his friend Homais for all the drugs he's taken from the pharmacy for Emma.
- To top it all off, Monsieur Lheureux is on *his* case now. The merchant tries to pull a fast one over on the poor doctor, claiming that Emma ordered two trunks instead of one, and demanding payment for everything. Lheureux threatens to sue if Charles doesn't pay up.
- The solution is not a solution after all: Lheureux agrees to accept a promissory note (a kind of fancy legal I.O.U. with interest) to be paid up six months later. Charles then has what he thinks is a brilliant idea – uh oh. He asks to borrow a thousand francs from Lheureux, which he will pay plus interest after a year. Lheureux, of course, agrees.
- Lheureux stands to make quite a profit from Charles's predicament. He hopes the doctor won't be able to pay up, so he can get in even deeper debt. We are starting to worry…a *lot*.
- Everything is looking up for the shady Monsieur Lheureux. He's feeling pretty good about himself.
- Charles, on the other hand, is feeling pretty darn bad, understandably. He doesn't know how he'll ever manage to pay back the merchant. The poor guy also feels guilty about worrying about money when he should be worrying about Emma full time.

Madame Bovary
Shmoop Learning Guide

- Emma slowly recovers from her shock.
- Winter arrives – it's a particularly harsh year. As spring approaches, her days fall into a dull, monotonous pattern.
- Father Bournisien starts to visit Emma, thinking that it's probably a good time for her to start praying.
- In her desperation, Emma takes great comfort in the priest's visits. At the peak of her illness, she asks for Holy Communion; when she receives the Communion wafer, she imagines an over-the-top, super-romanticized vision of heaven, which she then clings to. This is fascinatingly similar to the way in which she clung to the memory of Léon when he left – clearly she's using religion to fill the void left by romance.
- She resolves to become a saint.
- Father Bournisien is impressed by her zeal, albeit a little freaked out by it (he wonders if she's going a little mad – he obviously just doesn't know Emma that well). He has a variety of religious books sent to Yonville for Emma's edification.
- Emma attempts to read this odd collection of texts (one title we liked particularly is *The Errors of Voltaire, for the Use of Young People*); she doesn't really buy into all of them, but keeps gamely at them, believing herself to be the best Catholic *ever*.
- She puts her love for Rodolphe aside, and replaces it with an obsessive love of God, whom she addresses in the same way she used to address her lover. That seriously *can't* be right.
- Emma is in full religious overdrive for the moment. She devotes her time to charity, and is so docile that even her acerbic mother-in-law can't find a flaw in her. For the first time, she's actually kind and gentle with Berthe.
- In general, Emma seems like she and the world are getting along fairly well for the first time. Even the other housewives of the town accept her again and come and visit.
- The Homais children and Justin are also frequent visitors. Justin, we learn, is nurturing an intense crush on Emma.
- Emma grows gradually more and more introspective. She stops receiving visitors, and even stops going to church. Father Bournisien keeps visiting, but he mostly just hangs out with Charles and Binet (who likes to fish close by), drinking cider and chatting.
- Homais, of course, has a suggestion. He tells Charles to take Emma to the opera in Rouen, where a famous tenor is performing. The pharmacist is pleasantly surprised to see that the priest doesn't object; however, they quickly get into a fight about whether music is more or less moral than literature.
- Homais tries to involve Charles, who wants nothing to do with the argument.
- After the priest leaves, Homais again encourages Charles to take Emma to the opera. He brings it up with her, and insists that they go.
- The very next morning, the couple boards the Hirondelle and heads into Rouen. As usual, Homais bids them farewell, telling Emma she'll be a hit in Rouen in her pretty dress.
- Upon arrival in Rouen, Charles rushes off to get tickets (which he fumbles, but eventually resolves), while Emma does some shopping. Before they know it, it's time for the show to start.

Madame Bovary
Shmoop Learning Guide

Part II, Chapter Fifteen

- The opera is Donizetti's *Lucia di Lammermoor*, a tragedy in which an unfortunate heroine is driven mad because she's forced to marry the wrong man. Perhaps not the best choice for Emma…
- Emma and Charles take a stroll before the opera, and when they finally settle down in their seats, Emma feels satisfied for the first time in a long while. Waiting for the show to start, she admires her fellow audience-members.
- The opera immediately transports Emma back to the romantic novels of Sir Walter Scott she enjoyed as a girl (the opera was based upon book called *The Bride of Lammermoor* by Scott). She feels the music reverberate in her soul – it sounds like the old Emma is back.
- The famous tenor recommended by Homais, Edgar Lagardy, makes a dramatic entrance onstage. Emma is struck by his appearance, and the whole audience falls for him.
- Emma sees her own story in the narrative that unfolds before her. She thinks that nobody has ever loved her the way that the hero and heroine love each other.
- Charles doesn't really get what's going on, and he keeps bugging Emma with questions. She's not amused.
- A wedding scene unfolds on stage, and Emma thinks of her own wedding – she wishes that she, like the opera's heroine, had resisted and not married Charles.
- As things get more and more dramatic onstage, they also get more and more dramatic in Emma's mind. She imagines what it would be like to be the lover of Lagardy, the tenor. She is swept up in the fantasy of running away with the singer across Europe when the curtain falls; it's intermission.
- Charles runs off clumsily to get Emma something to drink. On his way back, he manages to spill the drink on a very upset lady, but makes it back to Emma somehow.
- Charles has big news. While he was away, he saw someone we haven't encountered for a while: Léon Dupuis.
- Before Charles even finishes telling Emma about his encounter, Léon himself shows up in their box. He and Emma shake hands and start catching up; just then, Act III of the opera begins.
- Emma is no longer interested in the drama onstage, now that there's some drama sitting right next to her. All of her pre-Rodolphe feelings start to return.
- Léon obviously feels something, too – he suggests that they leave the theatre and go elsewhere to talk. Charles, who's actually kind of into the opera now, doesn't want to go, but Emma insists.
- At a café, they eat ice cream and make small talk. Léon attempts to show off by discussing music – he claims that Lagardy isn't all he's cracked up to be.
- Charles, who's still bummed about missing the end of the performance, suggests that perhaps Emma might like to stay in Rouen by herself for a couple of days and see the opera again. Léon, of course, encourages this.
- Emma demurely makes no promises – she smiles oddly, knowing that something's up with Léon. She and Charles will decide overnight what she should do.
- The old friends part ways, with the clerk promising to visit Yonville soon.

Madame Bovary
Shmoop Learning Guide

Part III, Chapter One

- A lot of things happened to Léon in Paris. First of all, he studied law. Secondly, he studied women. He's no longer the same shy boy he was before. All along, he held on to a vague hope that someday he and Emma might actually get together, even while he had new experiences with other women.
- This new Léon is resolved to "possess" Emma. He's determined and much craftier than he used to be. He follows Emma and Charles to their inn, then returns the next morning to scout out the situation. He discovers Emma in the hotel room...*alone*.
- Léon has become something of a sweet-talker over the past few years. Perhaps he's not at the same level as Rodolphe, but he's getting up there. He and Emma talk and talk about the various sorrows of their lives. Sigh. Same old, same old.
- Noticeably, Emma doesn't say anything about loving another man, and Léon doesn't say anything about kind of forgetting Emma.
- Both of them make dramatic claims, each saying that life is miserable without the other.
- Basically, this love scene is just one big string of complaints – there's nothing romantic about that. Finally, Léon gives in and says out loud that he was in love with her.
- All of a sudden the tension is broken, and old feelings come rushing out, created anew by their current proximity. Emma is startled by how much she remembers – she feels old and experienced.
- They talk until night falls.
- Léon suggests that they could start over again, but Emma, attempting to be noble, says that she's too old and he's too young (they actually aren't that different in age, if at all).
- It's late – they've even missed the opera. Léon gets up to leave, but convinces Emma to meet him one more time. She makes their meeting point the famous Rouen cathedral.
- That night, Emma writes a farewell letter of her own, explaining to Léon why they can't be together. However, she can't send it, since she doesn't have his address. She decides to give it to him in person.
- Before the rendezvous, Léon primps nervously. He even buys Emma flowers, and goes to meet her at the cathedral.
- There, he's met not by Emma, but by a cathedral guide, who attempts to give Léon a tour.
- Emma's late, and Léon grows more anxious. Finally, she arrives. She starts to give him the letter, but is seized by the desire to pray. Léon is both charmed and irritated.
- As they're about to leave, the guide comes up and offers to give them a tour again. Emma, concerned for her virtue, desperately says yes.
- They follow the guide, not listening, through the cathedral and back to where they started. Before they get to the tower, Léon basically hurls a coin at the poor guide and pulls Emma away with him. The guide doesn't get the picture – he just keeps coming back. The couple flees the cathedral rather comically.
- Outside, Léon sends a little street kid to find a cab for them. Awkwardly, they wait alone – there's a kind of aggressive tension between them.
- The cab arrives. They get in as the cathedral guy yells at them from the church door, and Léon tells the driver to go wherever he wants.
- The following is one of the most famous scenes of the novel. We see the cab rushing through Rouen aimlessly; we can't see inside it, but we *can*, however, guess what's going on…Léon keeps yelling up to the driver to keep going; he and Emma stay concealed in the

Madame Bovary
Shmoop Learning Guide

cab.
- The poor cab driver is tired and certainly weirded out. His horses are exhausted, and everyone's demoralized. The passengers, however, give no sign.
- Around mid-afternoon, a hand is seen throwing scraps of paper out the window; we assume it's Emma bidding farewell to the well-intentioned farewell letter.
- Finally, in the early evening, the cab stops. Emma calmly steps out of it and walks away.

Part III, Chapter Two

- Emma returns to the inn, and finds that she's missed the Hirondelle, which was there to pick her up earlier. She hires a cab and catches up to the stagecoach. She returns home.
- Once there, Félicité sends her next door to the Homais house, saying that it's urgent.
- It's jam making day in Yonville, a particularly hectic time.
- At chez Homais, Emma discovers the pharmacist's family in an uproar. It turns out that Justin almost made a fatal mistake – he almost used a pan for jam that was dangerously close to the jar of arsenic.
- Homais is unbelievably angry; his wife and the children freak out, as though they'd already been poisoned. Emma observes all this, as Homais goes through the whole chain of events again.
- Poor Justin. Things just go from bad to worse for him. As Homais shakes him back and forth angrily, a book falls out of his pocket. Not just any book…a book called *Conjugal Love*. With pictures. The children are struck dumb, and Homais snatches it away furiously.
- At this point, Emma successfully breaks into the conversation. She asks what's wrong.
- Homais bluntly tells her that her father-in-law, the elder Monsieur Bovary, is dead.
- Emma goes to find Charles as Homais cools down a bit, still grumbling.
- Charles has been waiting for his wife, and tearfully greets her with a hug and kiss. Emma, remembering Léon, is grossed out by her husband. She responds with an extraordinary lack of sympathy.
- Charles, poor man, just thinks that Emma is struck by grief, when in reality, she just doesn't know what to say, and doesn't feel anything.
- Hippolyte limps in, bringing Emma's bags. Emma is embarrassed as ever by his presence, a symbol of Charles's failures.
- The next day, Charles's mother arrives. Mother and son are debilitated by grief; Emma is unmoved. Instead, she's daydreaming about Léon.
- Monsieur Lheureux, who seems to have an incredible radar system for knowing the absolute *worst* time for stopping by, stops by.
- The merchant and Emma step aside to discuss business. Lheureux slyly proposes another lending arrangement – knowing that Emma is a fool with money, he wants Charles to give her power of attorney (basically control over their financial situation), so he can deal with her.
- Soon enough, he returns with yards of black fabric for a mourning dress.
- Lheureux keeps pushing Emma about the whole power of attorney business, which she doesn't really understand. However, she figures things out soon enough.
- As soon as Charles's mother leaves, Emma goes into financier mode. She has a

Madame Bovary
Shmoop Learning Guide

- document drawn up by the notary, which gives her control over the family's money and loans.
- Charles is amazed by what seems like Emma's common sense. She slyly suggests that they should have someone else look over the notarized document before they sign it – and Charles himself sends her to Rouen to meet with Léon. She's gone for three days.

Part III, Chapter Three

- Those three days are like heaven. Emma and Léon stay in a waterfront hotel, doing nothing but enjoying each other's company. Emma is happier than she's been since Rodolphe.
- One day, on a boat ride, Emma is actually reminded of Rodolphe – the boatman mentions giving a ride to a gentleman of his appearance. She shudders, but gets over it quickly.
- The holiday has to end, though. Emma tells Léon to send letters to her to the home of Madame Rollet, the former wetnurse.
- As Léon makes his way home, having deposited Emma at the stagecoach, he wonders idly why she is so determined to get the power of attorney.

Part III, Chapter Four

- Léon is just as into the affair as Emma is. He reads her letters voraciously, and gets sick of his job; instead, he thinks about his mistress.
- One weekend, he misses Emma so much he actually visits Yonville. The townspeople are glad to see him. He stays in the Lion d'Or, Madame Lefrançois's inn, waiting for an opportune moment to see his love.
- On the second night of his visit, he's finally able to see her – in the same place she used to meet Rodolphe. They lament the difficulty of life…it's so hard to be apart!
- Emma gets more and more cunning; she meets with Madame Rollet to get her letters, orders tons of new items from Monsieur Lheureux, and even hatches a sly plan to get Charles to send her to Rouen once a week.
- Under the false pretenses of picking up her music again, she complains about her lack of skill with the piano. She wheedles Charles into agreeing to pay for lessons in Rouen.

Part III, Chapter Five

- Thursdays are Emma's Rouen days. She leaves on the Hirondelle at an ungodly hour of the morning, excited and anxious to see her lover.
- When she arrives, Léon comes to meet her. The two go to the same hotel room every week, and spend all day in bed, drinking champagne, eating, talking, and generally enjoying each other.

Madame Bovary
Shmoop Learning Guide

- Léon is enchanted both by Emma herself and by the idea that he has a real, live mistress.
- The end of their days together come fast, and each week they dramatically part. Before heading home in the Hirondelle, Emma gets her hair done in preparation for her return home.
- The stagecoach encounters a particularly unfortunate beggar on its trip – a blind man, whose horrifically infected eye-sockets are described in excruciating detail. Emma is afraid of him, though Hivert makes fun of the poor man.
- Charles is always waiting at home for Emma; she despairs on the inside upon arriving back in Yonville. She starts to care less about things at home, and never even yells at Félicité anymore.
- Justin still hangs around, attempting be useful, and cultivating his crush on Emma.
- The rest of the week passes in a haze of longing, until Emma and Léon are together again.
- In the safety of their hotel room, the lovers talk about their hopes, dreams, and fears; Emma admits to Léon that she has loved another man who left.
- Emma begins to think again about Paris, and wonders if they might be happier there.
- At home, Emma is extra careful to make Charles happy. Once, he almost finds something out – he ran into the woman that Emma supposedly takes piano lessons from, and she didn't know anything about Emma.
- Emma, afraid of being found out, makes up an excuse, then shows up later with a receipt for the lessons. From then on, it's just lies, lies, lies.
- Emma decides to take an extra hotel room in Rouen, just in case she encounters someone from the village in the city.
- One day, Monsieur Lheureux catches up to her, asking for all the money the Bovarys owe him.
- As always, he's thought of a temporary way out, through which he will certainly profit. He knows about a small piece of property Charles inherited, and encourages Emma to sell it. Since she has power of attorney, she has the right to do so. He's even lined up a buyer, a man called Langlois.
- The sale goes through quickly, and Lheureux assures Emma she did the right thing. She attempts to pay him back, but he instead gives her four more promissory notes.
- Oh no! Emma and Charles just keep sinking deeper and deeper into debt. This is getting scary. Despite the thousands of francs they owe the merchant, Emma orders a whole passel of new things. When presented with the bill, Charles ends up signing yet another sketchy promissory note.
- Charles's mom, who's visiting, bluntly states how foolish she finds this new round of purchases. She lets slip the fact that Charles has agreed to revoke the power of attorney he granted to Emma.
- Emma freaks out.
- For the first time, Charles rebels against his mother – at the worst possible time! She's the only one who demonstrates any common sense here, but Charles keeps defending Emma. His mother ends up leaving angrily.
- Charles, defeated by both the women in his life, has another power of attorney agreement drawn up to make Emma happy.
- Emma and Léon celebrate this renewal of her legal rights the next time they meet. Emma gets wilder and wilder – he doesn't understand what's going on with her, but he still finds her charming.
- One Thursday, Emma doesn't return to Yonville. Charles, a bit frantic, drives to Rouen

Madame Bovary
Shmoop Learning Guide

himself in the dead of night to try and find her. He runs around the city looking for her everywhere.
- Eventually, as he's about to go to the piano teacher's house, Emma herself comes out of nowhere, explaining that she was ill. Miraculously, Charles believes her.
- This incident actually gives Emma even more independence – she tells Charles that she can't feel free when he's always worrying about her. He gives her more space, which she promptly takes advantage of, heading into Rouen with the most ridiculous excuses every time she wants to see Léon.
- This recklessness starts to take its toll on Léon, however; his employers are unhappy with his constant absence. But he's easily led by his mistress, and he continues to escape work to meet her. He also does basically whatever she tells him to, from dressing all in black to attempting love poems in her honor (unfortunately, he can never come up with rhymes, and has to copy them).

Part III, Chapter Six

- On his many trips back to Yonville, Léon often has dinner with Homais, and thus feels obliged to invite him to come visit in Rouen. One Thursday, Homais unexpectedly takes him up on the offer.
- Emma is shocked to see the pharmacist waiting for the Hirondelle – he's excited about his trip to the city, and tells her all about his plans to revisit the places of his youth. Emma is not pleased.
- Upon arrival in Rouen, Homais dashes off to find Léon, and drags him into a café. They proceed to linger there for hours as Homais reminisces about the good old days.
- In the meantime, Emma is getting impatient. She waits for Léon all afternoon in their hotel room.
- Back at the café, Homais starts teasing Léon about his mistress. Worried that the pharmacist knows something, Léon plays dumb – it turns out that Homais thinks that Léon is in love with Félicité.
- This sets Homais off on a long diatribe about women. He goes on and on, as is his way, and Léon loses his patience. He rushes off, claiming to have an appointment.
- The pharmacist follows him all the way to the hotel. Léon rushes upstairs, and finds Emma distraught. He attempts to console her, but is called away again by Homais. He promises to return.
- Léon keeps trying to come up with new ways to get rid of the pharmacist. He says he has to work; Homais wants to come to the office. It's impossible to escape this man.
- Finally, Léon gives in to the pushy pharmacist, and they stop to visit a friend of Homais's. However, in the end, Léon manages to escape and run to the hotel – but Emma is gone.
- Emma decides first that she hates Léon, then that she's being too harsh on him. The pair reconciles, but things are different.
- In the following days, Emma and Léon's relationship sours. She still attempts to throw herself at him, hoping to find happiness again, but it's no use.
- Léon starts to wonder if Emma's going a little mad. She makes him nervous now, and he also starts to resent her domination. However, unfortunately for Léon, he still melts into a

Madame Bovary
Shmoop Learning Guide

little puddle of love every time he sees her.
- Emma actually *is* getting more than a little obsessive – she wants to know what Léon is doing all the time, and even thinks of having him followed.
- Nothing makes her happy anymore and, once again, she looks back on her life and wonders where it all went wrong. Sound familiar? It should – this has all happened before. Life seems hopeless once again.
- One day, the financial situation gets even worse – it turns out that Lheureux has turned Emma's debt over to one of his associates, one Monsieur Vinçart. Emma sends the messenger away, claiming that she'll pay up later. Unfortunately, the next day an official protest of non-payment shows up. Yikes.
- Emma runs to complain to Lheureux. He plays dumb, then attempts to shift the blame over to the mysterious Monsieur Vinçart. Emma leaves, somewhat pacified, and even accepts some fabric from the merchant (which, of course, she'll have to pay for later).
- Emma steps it up a notch, and figures out ways to get some money. The money from both Emma's and Charles's families has run out, so she starts billing patients behind Charles's back.
- She manages to limp along in this fashion for a while, paying off her debt in small portions, then signing more of those awful promissory notes. Clearly, Emma doesn't really get what's going on – when she tries to figure it out, she gets confused and gives up, which is *so* not the right thing to do.
- The house falls into disrepair; Emma snaps whenever anyone asks her about it.
- Poor Charles is still madly in love with Emma, and can't figure out what's going on with her. They don't even sleep in the same bed anymore – Emma stays in the bedroom, reading horror novels all night, while Charles is exiled to the attic.
- Emma's only happiness comes from her weekly escapes to Rouen. She still enjoys the luxury of the hotel room, and helps Léon pay for the room, despite her debts.
- He suggests that they might try a cheaper place, but Emma isn't down with that. They stick with the expensive hotel.
- To pay for this, Emma sells some of her things – she even asks Léon to pawn the fancy spoons her father gave her for her wedding. He's uncomfortable with this, and begins to wonder if his friends and family are right in telling him to ditch the mistress.
- Léon vows never to see Emma again, and this resolve diminishes her power over him. Now he's bored by her melodramatic outbursts.
- Just as in her affair with Rodolphe, Emma also feels the excitement go out of the relationship. She blames Léon, and wishes something terrible might happen so she can have an excuse to get out of their entanglement, but she's too cowardly to actually say anything to him.
- All the while, Emma imagines another ideal man, one made up of her assorted memories and desires, who can carry her away from her dull, humdrum life. Again, her fantasy world begins to consume reality.
- One Thursday, Emma stays the night in Rouen, partying it up with Léon and his friends at a masked ball. She is horrified by the company she finds herself in – the other women present are prostitutes. She faints, revives, then flees the party, disgusted with herself.
- Back in Yonville the next afternoon, Emma arrives home to a dreadful surprise: her house is being seized by governmental order! An official document had been sent the day before, demanding that she pay the whopping sum of eight thousand francs *within twenty four hours*.

Madame Bovary
Shmoop Learning Guide

- She doesn't believe it can possibly be true – the ridiculous enormity of the sum makes her think that it's just Lheureux trying to scare her.
- She goes to visit the merchant, confident that they can work something out.
- But Lheureux is not in a forgiving mood. It's payback time – literally. Emma realizes that this is serious business. She even tries to use her feminine wiles on Lheureux, but it's no use; he only wants his money.
- Lheureux heartlessly kicks Emma out of the office, desperate and helpless.

Part III, Chapter Seven

- The next day, the town bailiff, Maître Hareng, comes to the house to make an inventory of its goods.
- After they leave, Emma and Félicité try not to give anything away to Charles, who is somehow still blissfully ignorant of all of this.
- The government even sent a guard to make sure Emma doesn't do a runner; he stays obediently in the attic so Charles doesn't notice.
- The next day, Emma goes to Rouen to ask everyone she knows there for money.
- Finally, she comes to Léon's house. They go to their room in the Hôtel du Boulogne, where she proceeds to throw herself upon his mercy. However, he doesn't have eight thousand francs worth of mercy – who does?
- Léon attempts to tell her that things aren't as bad as she thinks – he claims that things will be fine if she pacifies Lheureux with a smaller amount, like three thousand francs. He obediently goes out for a while, supposedly looking for money somewhere, and comes back empty-handed.
- Emma, who's going off the deep-end right now, tries to force Léon to steal the money from his employer. Just when he's about to give in to her will, he remembers that his rich friend Morel will be back in town that evening – he promises to bring Emma the money the next day.
- But Emma is dubious, and Léon is uncomfortable. He was sure that Emma would believe this lie, but instead she doesn't look any better. He makes a quick exit.
- Wandering disconsolately through the town, Emma is almost run over by a passing carriage. She recognizes the man inside – it's the Viscount.
- She feels even worse than ever.
- On the way home, she encounters Homais in the Hirondelle, bringing home his wife's favorite rolls from a bakery in Rouen.
- They encounter the blind beggar, as usual. Homais is offended by this spectacle, and babbles on about what the blind man should do to cure his condition. Homais gives the beggar a coin, then actually asks for change (who *does* that?).
- Hivert, cruel man that he is, makes the beggar do a dog impression. Emma, full of pity and disgust, gives him a five-franc coin, all the money she has in the world. It seems like a noble gesture to her.
- Emma's feelings all desert her – she's just apathetic now. She hopes that something dramatic might occur – like Lheureux's death.
- Unfortunately, no such thing happens. Emma awakens to a commotion; a crowd is

Madame Bovary
Shmoop Learning Guide

- gathering in the town square where a sign has been posted. All of Emma's property is officially for sale.
- Emma and Félicité decide that the best course of action is to go to see Monsieur Guillaumin, the notary. It's a last ditch effort.
- The notary's house is elegant, and even in her despair, Emma notes that it's the type of house she should have.
- Apparently, Monsieur Guillaumin is secretly allied with Lheureux, but he lets Emma babble on about her financial troubles anyway. The notary calmly eats his breakfast while she tries to enlist his help.
- The only thing Guillaumin will accept in exchange for his help, it seems, is Emma herself. He makes a move on her as soon as she's done talking. Disgusted, she flees the scene.
- Back home, Félicité tries to help Emma think of people who can help – someone, anyone. Emma gives up, and imagines what she'll tell Charles when he gets home. She assumes that he will forgive her for ruining them financially – but she still doesn't forgive *him* for the supposed crime of ever meeting her.
- Charles returns, and Emma slips out before he sees her. She high-tails it over to Binet's, and presumably asks the tax collector if he can help (he can't).
- Two of the town's gossiping ladies, Madame Tuvache, the mayor's wife, and her friend Madame Caron, observe her, disgusted by her behavior.
- Emma, rejected by the whole town, flees to Madame Rollet's, where she has a small-scale nervous breakdown (understandably) and sends the wetnurse to see if Léon is at her house.
- In the nurse's cottage, Emma waits in vain for Léon, who never shows.
- Madame Rollet returns with bad news. Léon is nowhere to be found, Charles is crying, and everyone is looking for her.
- Emma only has one more place to go: she heads off to La Huchette to find Rodolphe, ready to giver herself to him for the three thousand francs.

Part III, Chapter Eight

- As she approaches La Huchette, Emma wonders what she can possibly say to her former lover.
- She finds Rodolphe in his room, smoking a pipe and sitting by the fire.
- Emma feebly attempts to win Rodolphe back, telling him that they can be together again. She looks beautiful in her despair, and he's actually moved – he kisses her and tells her she's the only woman for him.
- However, Emma picks this moment to confess everything, thinking that she's in the clear – she lies about how the money was lost, making it look like it's not her fault. She begs him for three thousand francs.
- Rodolphe is repelled by this outpouring of demands – he realizes that she only came to him for his money. He tells her honestly that he doesn't even have it.
- Rodolphe, despite his flaws, isn't a totally evil man. He would have given her the cash if he actually had it – however, he really doesn't.
- Emma doesn't believe this; she assumes that he never loved her, and that he's just

Madame Bovary
Shmoop Learning Guide

- holding out on her now. She flips out on him, accusing him of lying to her about his money. She uses his extravagant belongings as proof, and screams at him for everything he's ever done to her.
- Rodolphe asserts once again that he doesn't have the money. Emma, furious and desperate, leaves.
- It's nighttime; Emma's twenty-four hours are far past up, and she has nothing to give to Lheureux. On her way home, she stops at the pharmacy.
- The Homais family is having dinner, but she doesn't want to see them. The one she wants is Justin – she convinces him to give her the key to the poison cabinet upstairs, supposedly so she can kill some rats.
- Justin is awed by her beauty, and even though he feels something bad coming, he gives in. As soon as they get to the depository, she rushes to the bottle of arsenic that Homais pointed out on jam-making day so long ago, and begins to eat the white powder.
- Justin is totally freaked out, as he should be. He tries to stop her, but she threatens him, saying that everyone will think it's Homais's fault if he says anything.
- After ingesting the poison, Emma goes home, strangely satisfied.
- Charles is a complete mess. He doesn't understand what's going on at all – where could all this mysterious debt possibly come from? He goes out in search of Emma, and when he gets back, she's home already. He asks her brokenly what has happened.
- In response, Emma writes a letter and asks him to open it the next day. She goes to bed without another word.
- Emma observes her body's reaction with a detached calmness for a while – she assumes that she'll just go to sleep and not wake up.
- Death by arsenic, however, is not that easy. She awakens with an awful inky taste in her mouth, and is suddenly convulsed with nausea. The poison kicks in, and believe us, it's not pretty.
- At eight o'clock, Emma starts to vomit. Charles is confused by some of the symptoms, and can't tell what's wrong with her.
- Emma is wracked with violent convulsions. In Charles's terrified eyes, she finally sees the true love that she's never seen before – but it's too late.
- Charles desperately reads the letter and goes mad with desperation. Suddenly everyone knows that Emma has been poisoned; Homais sends Justin to fetch Doctors Canivet and Larivière.
- Everyone is freaking out. Homais tries his best to reason through what they should do, and Charles is useless.
- Emma finally realizes that Charles loved her all along, and she tries to soothe him – this only makes his grief worse.
- Berthe is brought in, tired and confused; the child thinks it's New Year's, the only time she's ever allowed to be up late, and expects presents. Soon, though, Berthe is terrified by her mother's horrible appearance, and is taken away.
- The symptoms seem to stop for a while, and Charles calms down, hoping that Emma will pull through.
- Canivet arrives, and decisively declares that Emma's stomach must be emptied. They give her a medication to induce vomiting.
- This turns out to be the wrong decision. Emma starts vomiting blood, and she begins to scream horribly. Everyone, even Monsieur Canivet, is horrified.
- Finally, Dr. Larivière arrives. With him comes a new infusion of hope – he's famous for his

Madame Bovary
Shmoop Learning Guide

- knowledge and skill, and everyone looks up to him.
- After seeing Emma, however, even Larivière is grim. Though he's used to seeing people in misery, he can't help but tear up at the sight of the distressed family. He tells Charles that there's nothing to be done.
- Homais, despite his grief, pulls it together enough to invite Dr. Larivière and Monsieur Canivet to lunch. Madame Homais quickly whips up the most extravagant meal she can find.
- Over several courses, Homais describes what he thinks happened to Emma. Nobody can figure out how she poisoned herself; Justin, overhearing this and undoubtedly feeling incredibly guilty, drops a stack of plates.
- Homais's pride soon consumes any residual concern he might have for poor Charles and Emma. He boastfully goes on an on about his knowledge of poisons and illnesses.
- Homais forces Dr. Larivière to check out all of his children to make sure they're in good health. Larivière, irritated, makes a snide joke about Homais, and attempts to leave. However, everyone else in the town had a similar idea; they mob the doctor, seeking his opinion on their various physical conditions.
- Larivière rolls off in his coach without seeing Emma again (he urges Canivet to stay with her), and the townspeople agree on the whole that the famous surgeon was pretty useless.
- Next, Father Bournisien shows up to administer the Last Rites to Emma before she dies. Homais goes with him, despite his cynicism about religion.
- Charles has one last moment of hope – it looks as though Emma is better after she receives the priest's blessing. However, this is just the calm before the storm.
- Suddenly, Emma is seized with a terrible convulsion, and her whole body is wracked with agony.
- From outside, the grating sound of the blind beggar's voice singing a crude song drifts in.
- Emma cries out, "The blind man!" and laughs hideously (III.8.110).
- She violently jerks back to the mattress, dead.

Part III, Chapter Nine

- Charles throws himself on Emma's corpse, overcome by grief. Homais goes home, invents a story about accidental poisoning to cover up the suicide, and writes it up for the newspaper.
- When he returns to the Bovarys' house, he finds Charles alone and frightened, Canivet having left him.
- Homais, with the best of intentions, attempts to distract Charles by talking about the weather.
- Father Bournisien succeeds in getting Charles to do something about the funeral. He makes extravagantly romantic plans – ones that Emma herself would have appreciated.
- Charles rebels against God; he curses the heavens for allowing this to happen.
- The priest and the pharmacist sit up with the corpse all night, holding a vigil for her. The whole time, they argue about religion.
- Charles's mother arrives in the morning. She attempts to reason with Charles about the expense of the funeral, and he actually stands up to her for the first time.

Madame Bovary
Shmoop Learning Guide

- The townspeople come to visit and pay their respects; they're bored, but each is unwilling to be the first to leave.
- Félicité is hysterical with grief. She, Madame Lefrançois, and old Madame Bovary dress Emma in her wedding gown to prepare her for her coffin. Grotesquely, a stream of black liquid flows out of the dead woman's mouth as they lift her.
- Homais and Bournisien continue their intellectual discussion.
- Charles comes in to say his final good bye in private. He reflects upon his memories of their past together, looks at her dead face, and is horrified.
- The priest and pharmacist lead him away. Homais shakily cuts a few locks of Emma's hair for Charles to keep.
- Félicité thoughtfully leaves a bottle of brandy and a pastry out for the men – Homais and Father Bournisien need no prompting to drink the alcohol. They part ways after finishing the bottle.
- Finally, after Emma's body is sealed inside three coffins, her father arrives. He faints immediately.

Part III, Chapter Ten

- Monsieur Rouault received a letter from the pharmacist after the fact – so Homais attempted to soften the blow by not exactly telling him that his daughter was dead. As a result, Rouault rode desperately to try and see Emma before she died – and arrived far too late.
- He and Charles cry together, and attempt to be strong for each other.
- The whole town turns out for the funeral, including Hippolyte and his fancy leg, as well as the dastardly Monsieur Lheureux.
- After an elaborate procession, Emma is buried by Lestiboudois. On the way back, Homais amuses himself by noting the improper behavior of his fellow townsfolk.
- After everything's over, Monsieur Rouault heavily says good bye to his son-in-law and the elder Madame Bovary. He immediately goes home to Les Bertaux, and even refuses to see Berthe, since she would make him even sadder.
- That night, Charles and his mother stay up talking. They make plans for her to move in, and she rejoices inwardly – she's finally defeated Emma.
- Rodolphe and Léon both sleep calmly in their respective homes, but those who loved Emma, Charles, her father, and Justin, stay awake, thinking of her.

Part III, Chapter Eleven

- After Emma's death, Charles and Berthe sink into greater and greater poverty. Everyone seems to want to get money out of poor Charles; Lheureux comes back for more, as does Emma's fake piano teacher, Mademoiselle Lempereur (who already got paid once for her collaboration, anyway).
- Charles refuses to sell any of Emma's belongings; as a result, he fights with his mother

Madame Bovary
Shmoop Learning Guide

- and she leaves.
- Félicité inherits all of Emma's wardrobe, and seeing her in those dresses makes Charles even sadder. Soon enough, she runs off with Théodore, Monsieur Guillaumin's servant.
- Léon, in the meanwhile, gets married and secures a post as a notary.
- Wandering through the house one day, Charles discovers Emma and Rodolphe's love letters. He is jealous, but still grieves intensely for Emma, regardless of her infidelity.
- In honor of her memory, he squanders his money on things she would have liked – fancy clothes and moustache wax. To pay for these things, he signs more promissory notes and goes into greater debt.
- Eventually, Charles has to sell everything and, after a while, all they have left is Emma's bedroom, full of her possessions.
- Berthe has nothing, and has nobody to care for her. Charles can't manage to actually take care of her.
- The Homais family breaks off their association with the Bovarys.
- Monsieur Homais turns his attention to civic matters. He manages to get the blind beggar shipped off to an asylum.
- This encourages him to expand his sphere of influence; the pharmacist goes on to write many more articles about local goings-on, and shifts his attention to writing a master work on his observations of Yonville. He also maintains his pharmacy, and keeps up with all the latest ridiculous developments.
- Homais and Charles choose an extravagant design for Emma's tombstone.
- Charles tries to keep the memory of Emma alive, but she fades from his memory. Eventually everyone, even Father Bournisien, gives up on him.
- Charles and his mother attempt to reconcile, but when she offers to take Berthe off his hands, they have a final decisive break.
- Charles is consumed with jealousy for Homais, who seems to have everything he wants. That is, everything but the cross of the Legion of Honor. The pharmacist makes it his top priority to acquire this prize. He starts to suck up to the local authorities.
- Finally, one day Charles discovers Léon's love letters in Emma's desk. Mad with fury, he rummages around everywhere and discovers a portrait of Rodolphe, as well.
- Charles totally breaks off communication with the rest of the town. Everyone assumes that he's a drunkard.
- He occasionally visits Madame Lefrançois to talk about Emma, but she doesn't have time for him.
- Finally, Charles is forced to sell his horse, the last thing he has. At the market, he runs into Rodolphe. They awkwardly have a beer together. Rodolphe talks about other things to avoid any discussion of Emma.
- In the end, Charles tells Rodolphe that he doesn't blame the other man, claiming that only fate is responsible for Emma's death.
- Rodolphe thinks of Charles as a pitiful, weak, meek man.
- The next day, Charles sits down in the garden. It's a beautiful spring day, and he's struck with emotion.
- Berthe comes to fetch him for dinner – but he's dead, the lock of Emma's hair in his hand.
- Berthe is sent away to live with her grandmother, who dies the same year. She's then passed on to a poor aunt, who sends the child to work in a cotton mill.
- Since Charles's death, three different doctors have all moved to Yonville to take over his practice. None of them succeed, due to the machinations of Monsieur Homais.

Madame Bovary
Shmoop Learning Guide

- Finally, the book closes as Monsieur Homais receives the cross of the Legion of Honor.

Themes

Theme of Dissatisfaction

Sometimes life just sucks. Hey, we didn't write the rules – it's true. However, in most of our lives, things are a series of ups and downs. Emma Bovary's life (of *Madame Bovary* fame) is no different. However, most of the time, she's stuck in "down" mode, and is never happy with what she has. Life always seems unfair to her, and she spends a good deal of her time thinking about how it really ought to be better. She's not the only one; most of the book's exciting characters aren't content with simply going with the flow and accepting life as it is.

Questions About Dissatisfaction

1. Do you think Emma could ever be completely happy? If so, under what circumstances?
2. Are any of the novel's characters totally satisfied with their lives?
3. How do men and women in the novel deal with their frustrations differently? How does society affect these coping mechanisms?

Chew on Dissatisfaction

Dissatisfaction is an essential element of ambition in the world that Flaubert creates.

Total satisfaction is available only to characters perceived as dull or unquestioning in *Madame Bovary*.

Theme of Freedom and Confinement

You all know the feeling of being trapped inside your own life. Well, take that to an *extreme*, and you've got *Madame Bovary*. The novel's protagonist feels stuck inside an unhappy marriage, a restrictive society, and a monotonous everyday routine, and she's willing do to almost anything to escape. She dreams of fleeing her old life and finding a new one that's more exciting and full of exotic possibility. However, every time she tries to change her life, it cycles back somehow into the same old, same old. Can she ever escape? Is escape even possible? The novel isn't very optimistic on that front.

Questions About Freedom and Confinement

1. Is Emma ever really "free?"
2. Emma perceives marriage as a prison. Does Flaubert offer any alternate models for marriage?
3. Does Emma's sense of confinement relate to her gender?

Madame Bovary
Shmoop Learning Guide

4. What role does money play in the theme of freedom and confinement in this novel?

Chew on Freedom and Confinement

Emma creates her prison through her own thoughts and actions.

The rigid expectations of the society that Flaubert depicts puts all of the characters under an equal amount of pressure; all of the characters are therefore just as confined by their circumstances as Emma is.

Theme of Foolishness and Folly

There are many, many poor decisions made in *Madame Bovary*. Really, it's so full of textbook BAD, *BAD* CHOICES that it could double as a manual of warning signs in a high school health class. We've got a whole range of folly here, from financial to emotional. The novel, however, makes no real moral judgments – instead, we just watch objectively as the characters get themselves deeper and deeper into trouble. The implication is that folly is a natural state of the human condition.

Questions About Foolishness and Folly

1. Is folly always a matter of action, or can *not* acting (like Charles) also be considered foolish?
2. Is it folly to simply indulge in one's imagination?
3. Does Emma ever realize when she makes a foolish decision?
4. Are all of Flaubert's characters in this novel fools? Are there any that can avoid this label?

Chew on Foolishness and Folly

Emma's greatest folly is her unshakeable belief in her own fantasies.

While Emma's actions in the novel are often perceived clearly as foolish, the novel does not judge them morally as right or wrong.

Theme of Love

Love encapsulates a whole lot of things in *Madame Bovary*. Seriously, just about everything relates to love: lust, beauty, power, money, fantasy – you name it. The thing is, nobody quite knows exactly what love is, which is why all these complications get tangled up in it. Our protagonist spends the whole novel going back and forth about whether she's in love, out of love, thinking about love, dreaming about love, worrying about love. In other words, it's a lot like modern day life.

Madame Bovary
Shmoop Learning Guide

Questions About Love

1. Can love be cultivated, or is it simply an inexplicable phenomenon?
2. Does Emma truly love either Rodolphe or Léon? Do they love her?
3. Is Emma capable of non-romantic love?
4. Do we see any examples of genuine love in this novel?

Chew on Love

In *Madame Bovary*, love and romance are incorrectly but inextricably identified with each other.

Emma is infatuated with the abstract idea of being in love, rather than the objects of her affections (Rodolphe and Léon).

Theme of Women and Femininity

Madame Bovary deconstructs the prim, idealized vision of the perfect nineteenth century woman, simply by giving her thoughts, feelings, and desires. Our protagonist is simultaneously the perfect woman and the nightmare woman of this period. She's beautiful, a good housekeeper, and on the outside seems like an obedient wife, but she's actually an adulteress, a spendthrift, and, to be honest, frivolous. Through the life of Emma Bovary, Flaubert attempts to show us an objective, intimate perspective on the difficulties of womanhood during a restrictive and judgmental time period.

Questions About Women and Femininity

1. Emma's concept of the ideal woman (which she strives to be) differs from that of the society around her. What do each of these images of womanhood look like?
2. Emma is continuously frustrated by her powerless position as a married woman, and wishes for a son. Do you think she would have loved a son more than she loves her daughter? Why?
3. How does Emma's view of womanhood and femininity relate to her upbringing? Do you think her ideas would be different if she had grown up with a mother?
4. How do the other women in the novel (Madame Homais, the elder Madame Bovary, etc.) reflect upon Flaubert's view of women in general?

Chew on Women and Femininity

Madame Bovary deconstructs the nineteenth century notion that women should have fewer desires and ambitions than men, and suggests instead that women's subordinate role in society creates greater tensions between their internal and external lives.

Instead of focusing on differences between the sexes, Flaubert comments upon the ways in which women and men are similar.

Madame Bovary
Shmoop Learning Guide

Theme of Wealth

Money, money, money – cold hard cash is certainly what makes this world go 'round in this novel. Underneath *Madame Bovary*'s concern for human emotion and feeling, the cruel truth is that money can make or break people. Even the most romantic characters are still driven by the desire for cash or luxury goods. The lust for wealth is like the pink elephant in the room; even when we think we're talking about love, joy, sadness or whatever else, money is always there in the background. In the end, it's also what drives the novel to its tragic conclusion.

Questions About Wealth

1. Does money equal happiness for Emma?
2. Do you think the wealthy people Emma encounters at the ball (and later Rodolphe) are actually happier than she is?
3. Emma is a big advocate of retail therapy. Do her purchases actually make her feel better?
4. Would Emma be content if she were married to a rich man?

Chew on Wealth

While Emma perceives wealth as the gateway to freedom, Rodolphe's character demonstrates that money doesn't necessarily buy true happiness.

In Emma's mind, wealth and luxury are necessary conditions for love.

Theme of Appearances

Appearance – and particular beauty – is always linked to power in *Madame Bovary*. People can have the appearance of wealth or refinement or sensitivity…and regardless of how false these appearances are, they are what get people places in this world. Our protagonist, Emma Bovary, is a beautiful woman, and her beauty has a profound effect over almost everyone she encounters. Because of it, she is able to change her life – and ultimately, ruin it. In the end, we discover what we should all know well already: people are definitely not always what they seem to be.

Questions About Appearances

1. Emma grows more beautiful as she gets deeper and deeper into trouble. Why do you think this happens?
2. Do we have clear pictures of the characters in the novel, other than Emma? Why or why not?
3. Does everyone in this society value appearance as much as Emma does?

Madame Bovary
Shmoop Learning Guide

Chew on Appearances
Emma's beauty is her greatest asset; it allows her to exert a degree of power over the men in the novel.

The greatest mistake that both Emma and Charles make in the novel is believing the people are exactly what they appear to be.

Theme of Repression
Madame Bovary is all about desire – and its consequences. The protagonist is tormented by her inexplicable, sensual yearnings, and her longing to escape from her small-town life. Her town is not exactly a forgiving place…nor was the nineteenth century exactly a very forgiving time. Social constraints impose a constant sense of tension upon the novel as a whole. This doesn't just apply to Emma Bovary herself; the whole society is so tightly wound that practically everyone is always hiding some secret desire. Once the façade of social boundaries cracks, though, *look out*.

Questions About Repression

1. Do you think the other townspeople have desires as wild as Emma's that they simply keep better hidden?
2. How much of Emma's desire is motivated by the temptation of the forbidden fruit?
3. What impact, if any, does society's rigid set of standards and demands have on Emma's decisions?

Chew on Repression
The intensity of social pressure increases Emma's enjoyment of her transgressions.

The romantic novels that Emma reads play upon the repressed desires of the society she lives in by glorifying adultery and other illicit activities.

Theme of Art and Culture
This may sound unusual, but art and culture are cause for worry in *Madame Bovary*. Emma Bovary, the novel's protagonist, is infatuated by the romantic novels she reads, and believes wholeheartedly in the vision of life she finds there. Similarly, she indulges emotionally in the other arts, such as music and painting. Some of the other characters worry that the dramatic emotions stirred in Emma are unhealthy; the blame mostly falls on the novels she reads. In the provincial world these characters inhabit, art and culture are seen as dangerous distractions, rather than necessities of life.

Questions About Art and Culture

1. Do you think the romantic novels that Emma reads actually have the adverse effect on her that Charles's mother claims?

Madame Bovary
Shmoop Learning Guide

2. Emma responds to art, literature, and music in an intensely personal, emotional fashion. Is there a right or wrong way to appreciate art?
3. How do the other characters' views on the arts reflect their personalities? Consider Charles, Léon, and Homais in particular.

Chew on Art and Culture

Emma is not corrupted by bad books; instead, she is corrupted because she is a bad reader.

The novel's distance from Paris, the center of culture, both fosters Emma's discontent and encourages her to create her own imaginary version of cosmopolitan life.

Quotes

Dissatisfaction Quotes

She had bought herself a blotter, a writing case, a pen and some envelopes, although she had no one to write to; she would dust off her whatnot, look at herself in the mirror, pick up a book, then begin to daydream between the lines and let it fall to her lap. She longed to travel, or to go back and live in the convent. She wanted both to die and to live in Paris. (I.9.13)

Thought: Bored with married life, Emma can't focus enough to commit to any hobbies. Her longing to live in Paris, which she thinks is the *only* place for her, is only rivaled by her melodramatic (and insincere) death wish.

[…] in the depths of her soul, she was waiting for something to happen. Like a sailor in distress, she kept scanning the solitude of her life with anxious eyes, straining to sight some far-off white sail in the mists of the horizon. She did not know how it would come to her, what wind would bring it to her, to what shores it would carry her, whether it would be a launch or a towering three-decker, laden with sorrow or filled to the gunwales with bliss. But every morning when she awoke she expected it to arrive that day; she listened to every sound, periodically leapt to her feet with a start and was surprised when she saw it had not come; then, at sundown, sadder than ever, she longed for the next day. (I.9.19)

Thought: Emma is certain that something great is destined to happen to her. However, day after day, nothing ever happens. We are forced to wonder how long she can maintain this futile optimism for…

This was the fourth time she had gone to bed in a strange place. The first was the day she entered the convent, the second was the day she arrived in Tostes, the third at La Vaubyessard, and now the fourth; and each one had marked the beginning of a new phase of her life. She did not believe that things could be the same in different places; and since her life so far had been bad, the remainder of it would surely be better. (II.2.17)

Madame Bovary
Shmoop Learning Guide

Thought: Reflecting upon her short life so far, Emma is sure that the worst is over (even though nothing particularly horrible has happened to her so far) – she's sure that her life is still waiting to really begin.

Léon was tired of loving without having anything to show for it; and then he was beginning to feel that dejection which comes from a routine life when there is no interest to guide it or hope to sustain it. He was so bored with Yonville that the sight of certain people and certain houses irritated him almost to the breaking point; and the pharmacist, good-natured though he might be, was becoming completely unbearable to him. And yet the prospect of a new situation frightened him as much as it delighted him. (II.6.34)

Thought: Emma's not the only dissatisfied one in this book. Dissatisfaction, it seems, not so terribly uncommon in small-town life. Léon, who is, like Emma, young, romantic, and a little foolish, has the same longing for something new, but is afraid to go out and get it.

What happiness there had been in those days! What freedom! What hope! What an abundance of illusions! She had none left now. Each new venture had cost her some of them, each of her successive conditions: as virgin, wife and mistress; she had lost them all along the course of her life, like a traveler who leaves some of his wealth at every inn along the road. (II.10.35)

Thought: Again, Emma finds herself at a crossroads. She's lost the optimism of her early youth, and now just feels a dull resignation.

This was how they wished they had been: each was creating an ideal into which he was now fitting his past life. Speech is a rolling mill which always stretches out the feelings that go into it. (III.1.15)

Thought: Upon their reunion, Emma and Léon both try to create new versions of the past few years, narrating things the way they *want* to see them, rather than how they really happened.

[Charles] seemed to her contemptible, weak and insignificant, a poor man in every sense of the word. How could she get rid of him? What an endless evening! She felt numb, as though she had been overcome by opium fumes. (III.2.35)

Thought: Emma is overwhelmed with disgust anew by Charles, after her blissful reunion with Léon. Her marriage is compared here to the dulling effect of opium…seriously not a good thing for any relationship.

She always assured herself that her next trip would bring her profound bliss, but afterward she would have to admit that she had felt nothing extraordinary. Her disappointment would soon be wiped away by new hope, and she would come back to him more ardent and avid than ever. She would eagerly throw off her clothes, pulling her thin corset string so violently that it hissed

Madame Bovary
Shmoop Learning Guide

like a snake winding itself around her hips. After she had tiptoed barefoot to the door to make sure once again that it was locked, she would let all her clothes fall in a single movement; then, pale, silent and solemn, she would fling herself on his chest and a long tremor would run through her body.

And yet, in that forehead covered with beads of cold sweat, in those stammering lips, those wild eyes and those clutching arms, Léon felt the presence of something mad, shadowy, and ominous, something that seemed to be subtly slipping between them, as though to separate them. (III.6.23-24)

Thought: Léon and Emma both seem to know that things are not right with their relationship – Emma tries to cover it up by simply trying to convince herself otherwise, but Léon can see the real cracks in the foundation.

The first months of her marriage, her rides in the forest, her waltzes with the viscount, Lagardy singing – everything passed before her eyes […] And Léon suddenly appeared to her as remote as the others.

"But I do love him!" she said to herself.

No matter: she was not happy, and never had been. Why was life so unsatisfying? Why did everything she leaned on instantly crumble into dust? […] nothing was worth seeking – everything was a lie! Each smile hid a yawn of boredom, each joy a curse, each pleasure its own disgust; and the sweetest kisses only left on one's lips a hopeless longing for a higher ecstasy. (III.6.29-30)

Thought: Yet again, Emma looks back, mourning the opportunities she lost. Now, her perspective is far more cynical than ever before: she's sure that no real man can offer her the ideal love she longs for.

She was now living in a state of profound and constant lassitude. She often received writs, documents bearing official stamps, but she scarcely even looked at them. She wished she could stop living entirely, or sleep continuously. (III.6.75)

Thought: This is where things start to really go downhill, fast. At the beginning of the book, Emma claimed to be so bored she could die, and we didn't believe her – here, though, we worry that she means it.

Freedom and Confinement Quotes

Emma was inwardly pleased to feel that she had so quickly attained that rare ideal of a pale, languid existence, beyond the reach of mediocre spirits. (I.6.10)

Madame Bovary
Shmoop Learning Guide

Thought: Even as a young girl, Emma feels the need to escape from the world of "mediocre spirits" – that is, everyone else. She prides herself on breaking free from convention.

So they were going to continue like this, one after the other, always the same, innumerable, bringing nothing! In other people's lives, dull as they might be, there was at least a chance that something might happen. One event sometimes had infinite ramifications and could change the whole setting of a person's life. But God had willed that nothing should ever happen to her. The future was a long, dark corridor with only a locked door at the end. (I.9.22)

Thought: Emma's life, now that she's stuck in a marriage, seems like it offers no possible escape, or even variation.

"Doesn't it seem to you," asked Madame Bovary, "that the mind moves more freely in the presence of that boundless expanse [the sea], that the sight of it elevates the soul and gives rise to thoughts of the infinite and the ideal?" (II.2.7)

Thought: In talking to Léon, Emma shares her views more openly – as though in conversation with him she feels the same freedom she describes here.

Sometimes, however, this hypocrisy became so repugnant to her that she was tempted to run away with Léon to some faraway place where she could begin a different life; but then she always felt as though some dark, mysterious abyss were opening up before her. (II.5.47)

Thought: The possibility of escape from Emma's marriage with Charles isn't a real possibility at all – she can't imagine what the alternative is.

The whitish light coming in through the windowpanes wavered as it slowly died away. The furniture, standing in its usual place, seemed somehow more motionless, and lost in the shadows as in an ocean of darkness. There was no fire in the fireplace, the clock was still ticking, and Emma felt vaguely amazed that all those things should be so calm when there was such turmoil inside her. (II.5.21)

Thought: Emma feels trapped by the simple stillness of her own house; she longs to burst out of it to a more active world.

Emma squinted, trying to pick out her house, and never before had the wretched village she lived in seemed so small to her. (II.9.26)

Thought: Riding with Rodolphe, the tiny world Emma lives in seems even smaller and more restrictive than she'd previously thought.

Madame Bovary
Shmoop Learning Guide

Nothing around them had changed; and yet, for her, something more momentous had happened than if the mountains had been shoved aside. (II.9.50)

Thought: After her first taste of freedom (the consummation of her relationship with Rodolphe), it feels as though Emma is in a new world.

"Just think what it will be like when we're in the stagecoach together! Can you imagine it? When the carriage begins to move I think I'll feel as though we're going up in a balloon, soaring up into the clouds." (II.12.36)

Thought: Emma anticipates the sense of freedom she longs for, and hopes to attain through her elopement with Rodolphe.

For Emma, there was something intoxicating in the sight of that vast concentration of life, and her heart swelled as though the hundred and twenty thousand souls palpitating there all sent her a breath of the passions she attributed to them. Her love expanded in that space, and filled itself with tumult from the vague clamor that floated up from below. (III.10.9)

Thought: Approaching Rouen, Emma feels a sense of possibility and excitement that contrasts markedly with the feeling of disgust and constraint she felt looking at Yonville from a distance.

Everything, including herself, seemed unbearable to her. She wished she could fly away like a bird and make herself young again somewhere in the vast purity of space. (III.6.82)

Thought: With the whole terrible wheel of debt set into motion, lonely and despairing Emma wishes she could escape the catastrophe that is her life – but of course, that's impossible.

Foolishness and Folly Quotes

[Emma] considered herself much more unhappy now, for she had experienced grief and knew it would never end.

A woman who had imposed such great sacrifices on herself certainly had a right to indulge in a few whims. She bought herself a Gothic prie-dieu; she spent fourteen francs in one month on lemons with which to bleach her fingernails, she sent for a blue cashmere dress from Rouen; she bought the finest scarf in Lheureux's shop. (II.7.5)

Thought: Emma is always sure that she knows best. Now that Léon is gone, her "grief" makes her feel like she's really lived life. However, this is just a ridiculous excuse for the retail therapy she indulges in.

Madame Bovary
Shmoop Learning Guide

"Don't you know there are some souls that are constantly tormented? They need dreams and action, one after the other, the purest passions, the most frenzied pleasures, and it leads them to throw themselves into all sorts of fantasies and follies." (II.8.40)

Thought: Here, Rodolphe attempts to tell Emma that her soul, one of these special ones that are always tormented, *needs* to give in to her desires – and to folly.

"I'm wrong, wrong!" she said. "I'm mad to listen to you!"

"Why? Emma! Emma!"

"Oh, Rodolphe," said the young woman slowly, leaning on his shoulder.

The broadcloth of her dress clung to the velvet of his coat. She tilted back her head and a long tremor ran through her body; weeping and hiding her face, she abandoned herself. (II.9.47-48)

Thought: Emma knows theoretically she's "wrong" and "mad" to give in to Rodolphe's advances, but she does anyway.

[…] she was becoming terribly sentimental. They had had to exchange miniatures and cut off locks of their hair, and she was now asking him for a ring, a real wedding ring, as a symbol of their eternal union. She often spoke to him about the "bells of evening" or the "voices of nature;" then she would tell him about her mother and ask about his. Rodolphe's mother had been dead for twenty years, but Emma kept consoling him in the affected language she would have used in speaking to a bereaved child; and sometimes she would even look up at the moon and say to him, "I'm sure they're both up there together, and I know they approve of our love." (II.10.28)

Thought: Emma, given the opportunity, shows that she still has the same silly ideas about romance that she cultivated as a kid. She's acting out the farcical part of a mistress in some trashy novel, and it makes her appear totally ridiculous to both us and Rodolphe.

[Monsieur Lheureux] talked with her about the latest items from Paris, about countless feminine novelties; he was extremely obliging and never asked for money. Emma abandoned herself to this easy way of satisfying all her whims. (II.12.12)

Thought: Sometimes we just want to grab Emma by the shoulders and shake her, yelling "Stupid! Stupid! Stupid!" This is one of those times. She just doesn't seem to realize that *buying* things means that you'll eventually be *billed* for them…

"What a fool I am!" he exclaimed, swearing violently. "Just the same, though, she was a pretty mistress!"

And Emma's beauty, along with all the pleasures of their love, rushed back into his mind.

Madame Bovary
Shmoop Learning Guide

For a moment he was deeply moved, then he rebelled against her.

"After all," he cried, gesticulating, "I can't go into exile and saddle myself with a child!" he told himself these things to strengthen his resolution. "And besides, all that trouble and expense […] Oh no! No, by God! That would be too stupid!" (II.12.58)

Thought: Rodolphe knows too well what the consequences of his actions are; he's a selfish man who would rather be a cruel heartbreaker than a fool for love. Though he's tempted to give in to emotion in the same wholehearted, vulnerable way Emma does, he knows better than to surrender to folly.

The sheets of the bed were sprinkled with holy water; the priest took the white Eucharistic host from the sacred pyx; and she was overcome with celestial bliss as she advanced her lips to receive the body of the Saviour […] She let her head fall back, thinking she heard the music of angelic harps coming to her through boundless space: and on a golden throne in an azure sky, amid saints holding green palm branches, God the Father appeared in all His majesty, motioning angels with wings of flame to descend to earth and bring her back in their arms. (II.14.5)

Thought: Now, don't get us wrong – there's absolutely nothing foolish about religion when people actually *believe* in it. Here, though, there's no real belief. Emma falls under the spell of a melodramatic, romanticized version of Catholicism, that she mostly constructs out of her own imagination, just like she did with her love for Léon or for Rodolphe.

Lying became a need, a mania, a pleasure; so much so that if she said she had walked down the right side of a street the day before, it was almost certain that she had walked down the left. (III.5.56)

Thought: Emma knows just how dangerous her situation is, but she's addicted to lying – it's become second nature to her.

Emma became a little confused in her calculations, and her ears were ringing as though gold coins were bursting open their bags and raining down on the floor all around her. (III.5.74)

Thought: Emma is not exactly the world's best accountant – instead of figuring out the financial mess she's created for herself, she just gets confused and bogged down by all the numbers, which, trust us, is not the right response.

Sometimes, it is true, she tried to make a few calculations, but she always ended with such exorbitant figures that she could not believe them; she would then begin all over again, quickly become confused, drop the whole matter and forget about it. (III.6.58)

Madame Bovary
Shmoop Learning Guide

Thought: Forget about it? Seriously? We have to wonder what exactly Emma thinks is going to happen here…everyone has to face the proverbial music sometime, after all.

Love Quotes

In her longing she confused the pleasures of luxury with the joys of the heart, elegant customs with refined feelings. Did not love, like Indian plants, require prepared soil and special temperatures? Sighs in the moonlight, long embraces, tears flowing onto yielding hands, all the fevers of the flesh and the languors of love – these things were inseparable from the balcony of a great castle in which life moved at a leisurely pace, from a boudoir with silk curtains, a thick carpet, filled flower stands and a bed mounted on a platform, from the sparkle of precious stones or the aiguillettes of liveried servants. (I.9.8)

Thought: Emma's view of love, influenced by the novels she reads, is tied inextricably to atmosphere – she feels as though she can't experience true love without the right setting, something of an odd and superficial claim.

Love, [Emma] felt, ought to come at once, with great thunderclaps and flashes of lightning; it was like a storm bursting upon life from the sky, uprooting it, overwhelming the will and sweeping the heart into the abyss. It did not occur to her that the rain forms puddles on a flat roof when drainpipes are clogged, and she would have continued to feel secure if she had not suddenly discovered a crack in the wall. (II.4.16)

Thought: Emma's misconception of love leads her astray. Preoccupied by her idealistic view of how love "ought" to be, she doesn't even recognize it when it creeps up on her gradually.

Then she asked herself, "Isn't he in love with someone? Who could it be? […] Why, it's me!"

All the evidence immediately became clear to her and her heart leapt. The flames in the fireplace cast a joyful, flickering light on the ceiling; she rolled over on her back and stretched out her arms.

Then began the eternal lament: "Oh, if only fate had willed it! Why can't things have been different? What would have been wrong with it?" (II.5.9-11)

Thought: In addition to being tied to setting, love is also interchangeable with drama for Emma. As soon as she realizes that Léon is in love with her, she has to immediately wail and moan about the cruelty of fate, as is customary in the novels she reads.

She was in love with Léon, and she sought solitude because it allowed her to revel in thoughts of him at leisure. His actual presence disturbed the voluptuous pleasure of her reveries. Her heart palpitated at the sound of his footsteps, but her agitation always began to subside as soon as he appeared, and she was left with nothing but deep astonishment which eventually turned

Madame Bovary
Shmoop Learning Guide

to sadness. (II.5.42)

Thought: Emma seems to be more in love with the idea of love than with Léon himself – she enjoys thinking about him, but not seeing him.

"Poor woman! She's gasping for love like a carp gasping for water on a kitchen table. A few sweet words and she'd adore me, I'm sure of it! She'd be affectionate, charming […] Yes, but how could I get rid of her later?" (II.7.36)

Thought: Rodolphe, a masterful manipulator of feelings, recognizes the symptoms of a romantic disposition in Emma, and understands her immediately. His view of love is not as idealistic has hers; instead, he cynically realizes from the beginning that their affair has a *very* limited lifespan.

She repeated to herself, "I have a lover! I have a lover!" and the thought gave her a delicious thrill, as though she were beginning a second puberty. At last she was going to possess the joys of love, that fever of happiness she had despaired of ever knowing. She was entering a marvelous realm in which everything would be passion, ecstasy and rapture… (II.9.58)

Thought: As Rodolphe's new mistress, Emma finally feels like all of the right circumstances have fallen into place (drama, passion, wealth) – she's ready to experience love for the first time.

[Rodolphe] made her into something compliant and corrupt. She remained under the influence of a kind of idiotic infatuation, full of admiration for him and sensuality for herself, a blissful torpor; and her soul, sinking into that intoxication, shriveled and drowned like the Duke of Clarence in his butt of malmsey. (II.12.23)

Thought: This description of Emma's love for Rodolphe is pretty repellent. Their love is not a respectful, beautiful mutual thing; instead, he treats her like an animal, and she, totally intoxicated by him, allows herself to be manipulated.

But disparaging those we love always detaches us from them to some extent. It is better not to touch our idols: the gilt comes off on our hands. (III.6.23)

Thought: Here, Flaubert touches upon a sad truth; once we start to pick out the flaws in the ones we love, they often lose their magic, and things start to fall apart.

[Léon] resented her continuous victory over him. He even tried to force himself to stop loving her, but as soon as he heard her footsteps he would feel helplessly weak, like a drunkard at the sight of liquor. (III.6.25)

Madame Bovary
Shmoop Learning Guide

Thought: Now Léon is the one in intoxicated thrall to his lover. Just as Emma was powerless in her relationship with Rodolphe, so too is Léon here. He's addicted to Emma, despite his longing to escape from her.

[…] she saw another man, a phantom composed of her most ardent memories, her strongest desires and the most beautiful things she had read. He finally became so real, so accessible, that she was thrilled and amazed, even though she was never able to imagine him clearly, for his form, like that of a god, was lost in the abundance of his attributes. He lived in that nebulous realm where silk ladders swing from balconies bathed in moonlight and the fragrance of flowers. She felt him hear her; he was about to come and sweep her away entirely in a kiss. Then she would fall back to earth, shattered, for these vague amorous raptures tired her more than the wildest orgies. (III.6.74)

Thought: Even after her carefully-constructed visions of love have been shot down, Emma continues to rebuild them, only now with a wholly imaginary lover at their center.

Women and Femininity Quotes

Would this misery last forever? Was there no escape from it? And yet she was certainly just as good as all those other women whose lives were happy! She had seen duchesses at La Vaubyessard who had dumpier figures and cruder manners than she, and she cursed God's injustice […] (I.9.36)

Thought: Emma is convinced that she deserves more than some of the rich women she saw at the ball, simply because she is more beautiful than they.

A man, at least is free; he can explore the whole range of the passions, go wherever he likes, overcome obstacles, savor the most exotic pleasures. But a woman is constantly thwarted. Inert and pliable, she is restricted by her physical weakness and her legal subjection. Her will, like the veil tied to her hat with a cord, quivers with every wind; there is always some desire urging her forward, always some convention holding her back. (II.3.12)

Thought: Women in Flaubert's day were far more restricted than their male counterparts, who were allowed to philander and experiment. Flaubert comments aptly here that women's desires can never be fulfilled in a society that holds them back.

And for a time she would be despondent and almost lifeless, gasping and sobbing softly with tears running down her cheeks.

"Why don't you tell Monsieur?" the maid asked whenever she came into the room during one of these crises.

"It's just my nerves," Emma would reply. "Don't mention it to him, it would only upset him."

Madame Bovary
Shmoop Learning Guide

"Oh, yes," Félicité said once, "you're just like the daughter of old Guérin, the fisherman at Le Pollet. I met her in Dieppe, before I came here. She was so sad! When you saw her standing in her doorway she made you think of a funeral pall hanging in front of the house. They say it was some kind of fog in her head that was bothering her. The doctors couldn't do anything for her, and neither could the priest. When it got too bad she used to go down to the beach all by herself, and sometimes the customs officer would find her lying face down on the pebbles, crying. Then after she got married it went away, or so they say.

"In my case," said Emma, "it didn't begin till after I was married." (II.5.48)

Thought: This is a rare moment between women. Flaubert doesn't show us much personal interaction between Emma and any other of the female characters (mainly because they're largely unimportant). However, here we get a glimpse into the communal lives of women at this time – Emma is not the only one who suffers from this kind of depression.

"Don't you know there are some souls that are constantly tormented? They need dreams and action, one after the other, the purest passions, the most frenzied pleasures, and it leads them to throw themselves into all sorts of fantasies and follies."

She looked at him as one looks at a traveler who has been in fabulous lands and said, "We poor women can't even enjoy that kind of distraction!" (II.8.40-41)

Thought: Rodolphe, here explaining to Emma why some people just have to give into their passions, can say this simply because he's a man. Emma, who longs to succumb to her passions but fears what will happen to her, envies him that freedom.

She remembered the heroines of novels she had read, and the lyrical legion of those adulterous women began to sing in her memory with sisterly voices that enchanted her. It was as though she herself were becoming part of that imaginary world, as though she were making the long dream of her youth come true by placing herself in the category of those amorous women she had envied so much. (II.9.58)

Thought: At this point, Emma's view of ideal womanhood is that of woman as lover – she's proud of her adultery, because it allows her to feel like a romantic heroine.

Her amorous activities changed her everyday behavior. Her glance grew bolder, her speech freer; she even had the audacity to walk with Rodolphe in public with a cigarette in her mouth, "as though she wanted to defy the whole world," people said. Finally even those who still had doubts lost them when she was seen stepping out of the Hirondelle one day wearing a tight, mannish-looking vest [...] (II.12.24)

Madame Bovary
Shmoop Learning Guide

Thought: Emma's rebellion exhibits itself in the most shocking way: what really horrifies the villagers is her adoption of masculine habits.

[…] in the pride of her devotion she likened herself to those great ladies of the past whose glory she had dreamed of while contemplating a portrait of La Vallière and who, majestically trailing the ornate trains of their long gowns, had withdrawn into solitude to shed at the feet of Christ the tears of a heart wounded by life. (II.14.9)

Thought: Emma's perspective on the ideal woman has changed here, after her break with Rodolphe. She now reverts back to a more conventional symbol, that of the bride of Christ.

[Léon] now savored for the first time the ineffable delicacies of feminine refinements. Never before had he encountered this grace of language, this modesty of attire, these languid, dovelike poses. He admired the exaltation of her soul and the lace on her petticoat. Furthermore, was she not a "lady" and a married woman – in short, a real mistress? (III.5.19)

Thought: Léon is enraptured by Emma's femininity; to him, she is the perfect woman, partially because she's the first real lady he's been close to.

There was a clerk, two medical students and a salesman – what company for her! As for the women, she quickly realized, from the sound of their voices, that most of them must be of the lowest class. Suddenly feeling afraid, she pushed back her chair and lowered her eyes. (III.6.78)

Thought: After years of thinking herself a member of some ideal, higher class of women, Emma comes to the brutal realization that she is perhaps no better than a common strumpet.

"Women like that ought to be horsewhipped!" said Madame Tuvache.

"Where is she now?" asked Madame Caron.

For Emma had disappeared while these words were being spoken. Then the two ladies saw her hurry down the main street of the village and turn right, as though heading for the cemetery, and they became lost in conjecture. (III.7.78-79)

Thought: In the tough world of Flaubert's microcosmic world, women aren't the gentle, sympathetic lambs his contemporaries made them out to be – instead, they're actually the most brutal critics.

Wealth Quotes

Madame Bovary
Shmoop Learning Guide

It seemed to her that certain parts of the earth must produce happiness like a plant indigenous to that soil and unable to flourish anywhere else. If only she could lean over the balcony of a Swiss chalet, or enclose her melancholy in a Scottish cottage, with a husband wearing a long black velvet cloak, a sugar-loaf hat and fancy cuffs! (I.7.1)

Thought: What Emma really means is that love and happiness, in her limited view, only flourish where the soil is, shall we say, *richer*.

Their clothes, better made, seemed of finer cloth, and their hair, brought forward over the temples in curls, seemed to glisten with more delicate pomades. They had the complexion of wealth, that white complexion that is heightened by the pallor of porcelain, the sheen of satin, the luster of fine furniture, and is kept in perfect condition by a moderate diet of exquisite foods. Their necks turned freely above low cravats; their long side whiskers descended to their turned-down collars; they wiped their lips with scented handkerchiefs bearing embroidered monograms. Those who were beginning to age seemed youthful, while those who were young had a certain look of maturity. Their faces wore that placid expression which comes from the daily gratification of the passions; and beneath their polished manners one could sense the special brutality that comes from half-easy triumphs which test one's strength and flatter one's vanity – the handling of thoroughbred horses, the pursuit of loose women. (I.8.21)

Thought: Here, Flaubert describes wealthy men as though they are a totally different species, unlike the common folk that Emma is used to.

Her trip to Vaubyessard had made a gap in her life, like one of those great crevasses which a storm will sometimes hollow out on a mountainside in a single night. But she managed to resign herself; she opened her drawer and reverently put away the clothes she had worn to the ball, including even her satin slippers, whose soles were yellowed from the slippery wax of the dance floor. Her heart was like them: contact with wealth something had left something on it which would not wear away. (I.8.51)

Thought: Now that Emma has seen what wealth is like, it has become an obsession. The ball plants the seeds of greedy desire in her heart, even though she knows it can never be satisfied in her everyday life.

In her longing she confused the pleasures of luxury with the joys of the heart, elegant customs with refined feelings. Did not love, like Indian plants, require prepared soil and special temperatures? Sighs in the moonlight, long embraces, tears flowing onto yielding hands, all the fevers of the flesh and the languors of love – these things were inseparable from the balcony of a great castle in which life moved at a leisurely pace, from a boudoir with silk curtains, a thick carpet, filled flower stands and a bed mounted on a platform, from the sparkle of precious stones or the aiguillettes of liveried servants. (I.9.8)

Bovary
ρ Learning Guide

Thought: Love and romance, in Emma's mind, are connected to wealth. The impression is that only rich people really know how to love, which is frankly just ridiculous.

Her carnal desires, her longing for money and the melancholy of her unfulfilled passion merged into one vast anguish, and instead of trying to distract herself from it she concentrated her attention on it, stirring up her pain and always looking for a chance to suffer. She complained bitterly about a badly served dish or a door left ajar, she lamented the velvet she did not own, the happiness that eluded her, her too lofty dreams, her too narrow house. (II.5.44)

Thought: Emma's longing for wealth ruins her enjoyment of life completely. Having seen how the other half life, she refuses to settle for anything less than opulence. Interestingly, she has a unique and unshakeable sense of entitlement that makes her believe that she deserves to be rich.

"Still, though," said Emma, "it seems to me you're scarcely to be pitied."

"Really?"

"Yes, because, after all, you're free…" She hesitated. "… rich…" (II.8.29)

Thought: Freedom is also connected to wealth for Emma. Basically, all the positive things in the world stem from money in her eyes. She can't understand why Rodolphe, a rich man, would ever be unhappy.

"Everybody can't be rich! Nobody has so much money that it can't all be squandered away! I'd be ashamed to pamper myself the way you do, even though I'm old now and need to take care of myself […]" (III.5.81)

Thought: Madame Bovary the elder makes an astute point – everyone runs out of money sometime. Emma, however, is never willing to listen to common sense when it comes to finances.

A wide porcelain stove was purring beneath a niche occupied by a cactus plant, and against the oak-colored wallpaper hung two pictures in black wooden frames. Steuben's Esmerelda and Schopin's Potiphar. The table, already set, the two silver chafing dishes, the crystal doorknobs, the floor, the furniture – everything gleamed with meticulous English cleanliness; the windows were adorned at each corner with panes of colored glass.

"This is the kind of dining room I ought to have," thought Emma. (III.7.48)

Madame Bovary
Shmoop Learning Guide

Thought: Even though she's in serious financial trouble, and is, in fact, at the notary's house to beg for money, Emma still can't help but long for the wealth she thinks she deserves.

She had begun to drift into madness; she suddenly felt afraid and managed to regain control of herself, although her thoughts were still in disorder, for she no longer remembered the cause of her horrible state: the question of money. She was now suffering only through her love, and she felt her soul slipping away in the memory of it, just as a wounded man, as he lies dying, feels his life flowing out through the bleeding gash. (III.8.22)

Thought: Again, we see wealth and love blend together in Emma's mind – in her desperation, she can't keep them straight. Was she at Rodolphe's for love or money? She can't tell.

Appearances Quotes

Emma, once so well-groomed and refined, now went for days without putting on a dress, wore gray cotton stockings and used cheap tallow candles. (I.9.57)

Thought: Emma's depression exhibits itself through her unusual lack of attention to her appearance.

Emma lost weight, her face became pale and gaunt. With her smooth black hair, her big eyes, her straight nose, her birdlike walk and the silence that had now become almost constant with her, did she not seem to be passing through life without touching it, bearing on her brow the mysterious mark of a sublime destiny? (II.5.40)

Thought: We can always tell how Emma feels through her appearance. Feeling separate and special, she begins to look that way, too.

The smooth folds of her dress concealed a tumultuous heart, and her modest lips told nothing of her torment. (II.5.42)

Thought: Emma doesn't betray her passions, and is able to maintain the façade of propriety, which apparently is all that matters.

"She's very nice, that wife of the doctor's," [Rodolphe] was saying to himself. "Beautiful teeth, black eyes, dainty feet, and graceful as a Parisian. How the devil did she get here? How did such a clumsy oaf ever get a wife like that?" (II.7.33)

Thought: Emma's looks are enough to make Rodolphe think she's out of place married to Charles in a place like Yonville – we see the power of her beauty here.

Madame Bovary
Shmoop Learning Guide

[Rodolphe] was dressed with that incongruous mixture of casualness and refinement which the common people regard as evidence of an eccentric life, tumultuous passions, artistic aspirations, and always a certain contempt for social convention, which either fascinates or exasperates them. (II.8.25)

Thought: Rodolphe's contrived appearance, a combination of wealth, eccentricity, and calculated style, immediately sets him apart from the "common people."

[…] when she saw herself in the mirror she was amazed by the way her face looked. Never before had her eyes been so big, so dark, so deep. She was transfigured by something subtle spread over her whole body. (II.9.57)

Thought: Emma's affair with Rodolphe seems to completely possess her body, and somehow transform it.

It was for [Rodolphe] that she filed her fingernails with the meticulous care of an engraver, faithfully rubbed her skin with cold cream and scented her handkerchiefs with patchouli. She wore all sorts of bracelets, rings and necklaces. On days when she expected him to come she would fill her two big blue glass vases with roses, arrange the whole room and adorn herself as though she were a courtesan awaiting a visit from a prince. (II.12.4)

Thought: Adultery makes Emma even vainer than she usually is; her appearance becomes her main occupation.

Madame Bovary had never been so beautiful as she was now; she had that indefinable beauty which results from joy, enthusiasm, and success, and which is essentially a harmony between temperament and circumstances. She had been gradually developed by her desires, her sorrows, her sensual experience and her still-young illusions, as flowers are developed by manure, rain, wind and sun, and her entire nature was now in bloom. Her eyelids seemed to have been made expressly for those long amorous glances in which her pupils were lost in profound reverie while her heavy breathing dilated her thin nostrils and raised the fleshy corners of her lips, with their delicate shadow of dark down. Her twisted hair seemed to have been arranged by some artist skilled in corruption; it lay coiled in a heavy mass, carelessly shaped by the adulterous embraces that loosened it every day. Her voice now took on softer inflections, and so did her body, even the folds of her dress and the arch of her foot gave off a kind of subtle, penetrating emanation. (II.12.36)

Thought: Somehow, Emma's body channels her emotions yet again; everything about her is sensuous, luxuriant, and incredibly sexy, even the fabric of her dress.

**Madame Bovary
Shmoop Learning Guide**

With the diversity of her moods – by turns mystic, joyous, loquacious, taciturn, passionate or nonchalant – she awakened a thousand desires in him, aroused his instincts and memories. She was the amorous heroine of all novels and plays, the vague "she" of all poetry. He saw in her shoulders the amber skin of the "Bathing Odalisque"; she had the long-waisted figure of a feudal chatelaine; she also resembled the "Pale Woman of Barcelona," but above all she was an angel! (III.5.20)

Thought: To the smitten Léon, Emma takes on the appearance of his artistic ideals; he reads his vision of the perfect woman into her.

[Léon's] soul was carried away by her sweet words and kisses. Where had she learned that depravity, so profound and so artfully concealed that it was almost intangible? (III.5.107)

Thought: Again, we see how well Emma hides her inner state with her beautiful exterior – this juxtaposition grows more and more menacing.

She looked extraordinarily beautiful to him, and majestic as a phantom; without understanding what she wanted, he had a foreboding of something terrible. (III.8.28)

Thought: Emma's beauty, heightened by her desperation, gives her a menacing power over Justin; again, we see her appearance impact those around her with an astonishing strength.

Repression Quotes

Metaphorical expressions such as "betrothed," "spouse," "heavenly lover," and "eternal wedlock," which constantly recur in sermons, stirred previously unknown depths of sweet emotion in her soul. (I.6.4)

Thought: As a young girl in the convent school, all of Emma's fledgling physical desires are channeled into her religious fervor, and not allowed to exhibit themselves in any way.

She played boldly, sweeping up and down the keyboard without faltering. Thus shaken by her vigorous touch, the old instrument, whose strings jangled, could be heard at the other end of the village if the window was open [...] (I.7.6)

Thought: All of Emma's aggression, given no other outlet, is unleashed upon the unfortunate old piano.

The housewives all admired [Emma] for her thriftiness, Charles's patients for her courtesy, the poor for her generosity.

Yet she was full of covetous desires, anger and hatred. The smooth folds of her dress

Madame Bovary
Shmoop Learning Guide

concealed a tumultuous heart, and her modest lips told nothing of her torment. She was in love with Léon, and she sought solitude because it allowed her to revel in thoughts of him at leisure. (II.5.41-42)

Thought: Here, Emma demonstrates her ability to go along with society's rules on the surface, while she thinks naughty thoughts on the inside. We have to wonder how long she can keep up this tense dual life.

[…] the more clearly aware of her love she became, the more she tried to repress it in order to conceal and diminish it. She wished Léon would guess it, and she imagined chance circumstances that would have facilitated its consummation. She was no doubt held back by indolence or fear, and also by shame. She felt that she had kept him at too great a distance, that it was now too late, that all was lost. Furthermore, the pride and pleasure she felt when she said to herself "I'm virtuous," or watched herself in the mirror as she struck various poses of resignation, consoled her a little for the sacrifice she thought she was making. (II.5.43)

Thought: Emma is torn here between pain and pleasure; she is pleased by her sense of self-sacrifice, but longs for an expression of the feelings she's bottled up inside.

The drabness of her daily life made her dream of luxury, her husband's conjugal affection drove her to adulterous desires. She wished he would beat her so that she could feel more justified in hating him and taking vengeance upon him. She was sometimes amazed by the horrible conjectures that came into her mind; and yet she had to go on smiling, hearing herself told over and over that she was lucky, pretending to be happy, letting everyone believe it! (II.5.46)

Thought: Everyone else's insistence that Emma has a great life drives her crazy – but there's nothing she can do about it. The thing is, she *does* theoretically have everything that should make a woman happy…she's not *supposed* to have the desires that torment her, according to the rules of society.

She cursed herself for not having surrendered to her love for Léon; she thirsted for his lips. She longed to suddenly run after him, to throw herself in his arms and say to him, "Here I am: I'm yours!" But she was discouraged in advance by the difficulties of such an action, and her desire, augmented by regret, became all the more intense. (II.7.2)

Thought: Here, we see that repression just makes desires grow even hotter – being denied something makes Emma want it more.

Rodolphe had moved nearer to Emma and was now saying softly and rapidly, "Aren't you disgusted by the way society conspires against us? Is there a single feeling they don't condemn? The noblest instincts and the purest affinities are persecuted and slandered, and if two poor hearts manage to find each other, everything is organized to keep them apart. They'll try anyway, though: they'll beat their wings and call out to each other. And you can be sure of

Madame Bovary
Shmoop Learning Guide

this: sooner or later, in six months or ten years, they'll come together and bring their love to fruition, because fate requires it and they were born for each other." (II.8.45)

Thought: Here, Rodolphe basically tells Emma that they're bound to get together, regardless of her marriage and the scandal it would cause. We get the feeling that he doesn't really believe in all of this "love will conquer all" stuff – he just says it to get her to turn against the restrictive rules of the society she lives in.

She did not know whether she regretted having given in to him or whether, instead, she wished she could love him more. Her humiliating awareness of her own weakness was turning into resentment, which was tempered by her voluptuous pleasures. It was not an attachment, it was a kind of continuous seduction. She was under his domination. She was almost afraid of him. (II.10.33)

Thought: Emma's domination by social convention has been replaced by a new domination – by her lover. Even as she sought to free herself from the oppressive constraints of society, she is still not at liberty to do as she likes, since Rodolphe now controls her emotions and desires.

[Léon] did not understand the deep-seated reaction that was now driving her into a still more reckless pursuit of sensual pleasure. She was becoming more and more excitable, greedy and voluptuous; and she walked with him in the street with her head high, unafraid, she said, of compromising herself. (III.5.93)

Thought: Once Emma breaks enough of the rules and continues to get away with it, she can't go back – instead, she gets more and more reckless.

Art and Culture Quotes

Endless sarabands ran through her head and, like dancing girls on a flowered carpet, her thoughts skipped with the notes, moving from dream to dream, sorrow to sorrow. (I.9.31)

Thought: Emma comforts herself with whatever artistic outlets she can find – even when the best she can do is the beggar with the hurdy-gurdy. She doesn't distinguish between highbrow and lowbrow.

Emma went on: "And what kind of music do you prefer?"

"Oh, German music, the kind that makes you dream." (II.2.10)

Thought: With this statement, Léon establishes himself as Emma's equal – someone who experiences art the same personal (and super-romantic) way that she does.

Madame Bovary
Shmoop Learning Guide

"What could be better than to sit beside the fire at night with a book and a glowing lamp while the wind beats against the windows [...] Your mind is free then," [Léon] went on. "The hours pass, and, without leaving your chair, you wander through countries that are clearly visible to you. Your imagination is caught up in the story and you see all the details, experience all the adventures; it seizes the characters and you have the feeling that you are living in their costumes." (II.2.10)

Thought: Again, Léon unknowingly emphasizes their similarities by describing precisely the way that Emma reads books.

"I hate commonplace heroes and lukewarm emotions, the kind you find in real life." (II.2.10)

Thought: Emma boldly states her view of art and literature: she's only interested in it as an escapist endeavor.

"Do you know what your wife needs?" said the elder Madame Bovary. "She needs hard work, with her hands! If she had to work for a living, like so many other people, she wouldn't have those vapors; they come from the silly ideas she fills her head with, and the idle life she leads."

"But she's busy a good part of the time already," said Charles.

"Oh, busy! Busy doing what? Reading novels and other bad books that are against religion and make fun of priests with quotations from Voltaire! It can lead to all kinds of things, my son – a person who isn't religious always comes to a bad end."

It was therefore decided to keep Emma from reading novels. (II.7.14)

Thought: Mama Bovary and Charles decide that it's the books that have ruined Emma – thus openly expressing an anti-intellectual, anti-artistic undercurrent that Flaubert depicts in this middle-class society all the way through the novel.

"I know very well," objected the priest, "that there are good literary works and good authors. But all those people of different sex gathered in a luxurious room decorated with all sorts of worldly splendor, and the pagan disguises, the make-up, the bright lights, the effeminate voices – those things alone are enough to create a licentious frame of mind and give rise to evil thoughts and impure temptations. At least that's the opinion of all the Fathers of the Church... And if the Church condemned the theater," he added [...] "she must have had good reasons for it." (II.14.19)

Thought: Father Bournisien attempts to paint a malicious picture of the theatre as a den of sin, but he just comes off as being rather ridiculous.

Madame Bovary
Shmoop Learning Guide

[...] the elusive thoughts that came back into her mind were quickly dispersed by the overwhelming flow of the music. She abandoned herself to the soaring melodies and felt herself migrating to the depths of her being, as though the violin bows were being drawn across her nerves. (II.15.6)

Thought: Emma *feels* the music much more than the average listener – she feels as though she is a part of it. This is analogous to the intensely personally way in which she reads books and looks at paintings.

She filled her heart with the melodious laments as they slowly floated up to her accompanied by the strains of the double basses, like the cries of a castaway in the tumult of a storm. She recognized all the ecstasy and anguish that had once nearly brought on her death. Lucia's voice seemed only the echo of her own heart, and the illusion that was now holding her in its spell seemed a part of her own life. (II.15.8)

Thought: Emma surrenders herself totally to the opera, and over-identifies with Lucia. Rather than being able to appreciate the music for what it is, she inserts herself completely into it, losing her hold on reality.

She was the amorous heroine of all novels and plays, the vague "she" of all poetry. He saw in her shoulders the amber skin of the "Bathing Odalisque"; she had the long-waisted figure of a feudal chatelaine; she also resembled the "Pale woman of Barcelona," but above all she was an angel! (III.5.20)

Thought: Léon's visions of the ideal woman are based on works of art; to make Emma fit his mold of the perfect woman, he superimposes them onto her.

[Léon] was about to be promoted to head clerk; it was time to settle down and work hard. He therefore gave up the flute, exalted sentiments and flights of fancy – for every bourgeois, in the heat of his youth, if only for a day or a minute, has believed himself capable of stormy passions and lofty enterprises. (III.6.70)

Thought: In the end, even good ol' Léon is forced to give up his artistic aspirations in the name of real-life practicality…only Emma holds on to her extravagant romantic fantasies.

Plot Analysis

Classic Plot Analysis

Initial Situation

Madame Bovary
Shmoop Learning Guide

Emma and Charles Bovary establish their married life
We meet Charles, then Emma and, soon enough, we see them set up their first household in Tostes. Everything may seem peachy from the outside, but we can sense trouble coming. Charles is all like, "Whoohoo! Marriage is awesome!" while Emma's feelings are more along the lines of "Meh." This is never a good sign for a relationship.

Conflict
Emma gets her first taste of the good life at the Comte d'Andervilliers' ball
Uh oh. Just as we'd feared, Emma is not going to give in and settle with her small-town life – at least, not without a fight. She's encouraged by a visit to the palatial home of the Comte d'Andervilliers, where she learns that some people do live the opulent life she dreams of.

Complication
Léon enters the picture; Emma begins to wonder about having an affair
With the appearance of an eligible, romantic, adequately handsome young man, Emma suddenly has something to be excited about. We've already seen how easily encouraged she is – and this new development leads her to believe that her fantasy life is actually closer than she'd previously thought. She ponders taking action, like running away with Léon, but doesn't actually do anything about it.

Climax
Emma gives in to her desires and starts her affair with Rodolphe
Léon is out of the picture, but Rodolphe shows up soon enough – and it doesn't take him long to convince Emma to become his mistress. This is an important tipping-point; after she gives in to Rodolphe's advances, Emma's character changes. Instead of just wishing that things would happen, she begins to *make* them happen, by whatever means possible.

Suspense
Léon and Emma's affair resumes and gets riskier and riskier…
After their awkward reunion at the opera, Emma and Léon finally get their feelings out in the open. Emma, whose tendency towards recklessness we already witnessed in her affair with Rodolphe, becomes truly foolhardy, taking risks that make our blood pressure rise. Her lack of caution is notable, not only in her relationship with Léon, but in her financial decisions. The novel is clearly building to some kind of fever pitch here.

Denouement
Monsieur Lheureux demands his money; Emma despairs
That fever pitch we mentioned? This is it. Everything in Emma's life comes crashing down around her when Monsieur Lheureux sends a collection agency after her. Her shock and desperation mount as she attempts to find the payback money – suddenly, all the mistakes she made earlier are back with a vengeance. Instead of everything working out, as it usually does in a novel's denouement, all of Emma's problems present themselves with renewed strength.

Conclusion
Emma commits suicide; Charles consequently dies
You can't get any more conclusive than this resolution: practically everyone is dead. Though it's final, it's certainly not clear-cut; though Emma dies due to her own foolish actions, we

Madame Bovary
Shmoop Learning Guide

don't necessarily condemn her, and even though Charles's neglect of Berthe verges on criminal, we don't judge him, either. Righteous morality would have been the easy way out for this novel – but Flaubert doesn't take that route. Instead, he allows us, the readers, to see the impact that the actions of a single person can have on the lives of others, and make our own decisions about it.

Booker's Seven Basic Plots Analysis: Tragedy

Anticipation Stage
Emma and Charles set up their married household, first in Tostes, then in Yonville.
Things are nice and smooth on the surface of this marriage, but we can see that Emma's frustrations are reaching a peak. It seems as though it's only a matter of time before she busts out and does something to shake things up. However, at this point, it could go either way – we're not sure this story is going to end in tragedy.

Dream Stage
Emma and Charles set up their married household, first in Tostes, then in Yonville.
Things are nice and smooth on the surface of this marriage, but we can see that Emma's frustrations are reaching a peak. It seems as though it's only a matter of time before she busts out and does something to shake things up. However, at this point, it could go either way – we're not sure this story is going to end in tragedy.

Dream Stage
Emma embarks upon her affairs with Rodolphe and Léon.
Emma's Dream Stage is kind of a bumpy one; she goes through ups and downs based on how her affairs are going. However, when they're good, they're very good, and she's flying high. When she's really smitten with both Rodolphe and Léon, she's incredibly happy, and she maintains the illusion that this stage can last forever. Unfortunately, we see her come down from both of these relationships fairly soon – clearly, Emma is only interested in that honeymoon period of swoony, over-the-top romance, and not in actual relationships.

Frustration Stage
Emma realizes that her affairs can never stay sufficiently exciting – she and Léon begin to lose interest in each other.
Emma comes to realize what we've seen all along: she really isn't good at sustaining relationships. She and Léon start to get bored with one another, and despite the fact that she's still trying to make things work out with him, she constructs another dream man in her imagination, hoping that someday he'll come along and make everything right. Meanwhile, Emma starts to feel worse and worse about her real-life entanglement with Léon, culminating in a horrible experience she has at an all night party (when she realizes that she's the only woman there who's not a prostitute).

Nightmare Stage
Returning home from Rouen one day, Emma receives notice that she owes Monsieur Lheureux 8,000 francs. She desperately tries to get the money from everyone she knows, to no avail.

Madame Bovary
Shmoop Learning Guide

All of Emma's previous mistakes have come back to bite her in the butt. This really is like a terrible nightmare – she's forced to prostrate herself before all of the men in her life and beg for money. Suddenly, it seems as though that fantasy life that she'd been living has just been a cover for the disaster that's her real life. Bad thing upon bad thing pile up, and Emma doesn't know what she can possibly do to pay Lheureux back in time. There is something truly horrifying about the speed with which Emma's whole life unravels.

Death Wish Stage
After failing to get any of her payback money, Emma eats arsenic and dies in agony. In the aftermath of the suicide, her family falls apart.
Left with nobody else to turn to (except Charles, who she can't face), Emma decides to commit suicide. She doesn't realize that consuming rat poison will put her through unspeakable torments – she thinks she'll just fall asleep and not wake up. We can't tell how clearly Emma makes this decision; it all happens so fast that we almost can't believe it. Abandoned by her lovers and pursued by creditors, she is sure that nothing else can possibly help her resolve her troubles. However, this is a totally selfish move on her part, since she doesn't consider the fact that she's leaving Charles saddled with her debts, as well as with their child.

Three Act Plot Analysis

Act I
Part I: Flaubert has actually divided his novel into three appropriate sections for us. This first one ends as Emma's depression and discontentment motivates the move from Tostes.

Act II
Part II: Emma begins to wonder about experimenting with life outside marriage; she falls in love with Léon, but actually embarks upon an adulterous affair with Rodolphe. This "act" finishes with her reunion with Léon.

Act III
Part III: Emma starts her affair with Léon, but things quickly spin out of control, both emotionally and financially, and end in ruin.

Study Questions

1. What claims does *Madame Bovary* make for the role of women in the society of Flaubert's time?
2. How does the novel's narrative voice contribute to its effectiveness?
3. How sympathetic (or unsympathetic) are we to the novel's main characters? How does this affect our reading of the novel?
4. Is Emma believable as a real woman, rather than simply a literary character?
5. What do you think Flaubert meant when he declared, "Madame Bovary, c'est moi" (I am

**Madame Bovary
Shmoop Learning Guide**

Madame Bovary)?

Characters

All Characters

Emma Bovary Character Analysis

So, the book is called *Madame Bovary*. It's pretty straightforward. The book really *is* Madame Bovary; without Emma, it's nothing. She provides its plot, much of its perspective, and she is the absolute center of the novel at all times. For this reason, we can't really hate her, despite her many flaws. Sure, she can be selfish, greedy, arrogant, and totally irrational…but we still don't give up on her entirely. We're so involved in Emma's inner life that it's impossible to totally write her off.

This is the genius of Flaubert's book: in Emma, he creates a character that's so real and so amazingly close to us that she *can't* totally alienate us, no matter what she does, and no matter how often he skewers her romantic ideas and roasts them on the fires of sarcasm. Heck, even after she pushes her own poor little infant child to the ground, we still go back for more. We don't exactly *forgive* Emma for the things she does, but we stick with her story to the end, regardless of how we feel about her actions. By the novel's end, we feel like we know her pretty darn well. But what *do* we really know about her? Let's explore some aspects of her personality…

Emma the Dreamer
Sometimes it seems like Emma's "real" life is actually the one she lives in her imagination. She's a compulsive dreamer, and she truly seems to believe that the fantasy worlds she experiences in novels should be – and can be – real, given the right resources (as in, vast wealth). The problem with Emma's active imaginary life is that it doesn't quite jive with the world outside her mind; she simply refuses to believe that her idealistic, unrealistic, and childishly romantic conceptions of things like love, marriage, and, well, life in general aren't real. The vast difference between the world she longs to live in and the world she *actually* lives in gradually makes her bitter and cynical, but no wiser.

Emma the Wife
Though Emma is fully capable of being a good wife and responsible mother on the outside, she just refuses to acknowledge that that's all her life is destined to be. She genuinely feels as though her marriage with Charles is what ruined her entire life, and blames him for ever coming along and marrying her. She periodically settles down and attempts (often with adequate results) to be docile and domestic, but it never really catches hold – she always drifts off and wonders what other directions her life could go in.

Madame Bovary
Shmoop Learning Guide

What really disturbs Emma about married life is how consistent it is – which proves that she could never have been happy, regardless of who she married, or where she lived. The constant sense of intrigue and excitement she longs for is difficult to sustain in any walk of life, but she's sure that it's marriage that's keeping her down. The baby, Berthe, makes matters even worse – Emma feels even more pressured and entrapped by the child, and has difficulty mustering up even the slightest smidgeon of genuine affection for the poor kid.

Emma the Mistress
In an attempt to board the thrilling, non-stop-roller-coaster of Life that she hopes to ride all the way to Unending Bliss, Emma becomes an enthusiastic mistress, first to Rodolphe, then to Léon. However, even adultery isn't satisfactory for her after a while. The initial thrill of cheating gives way to the anxieties and nerve-wracking tensions of…well,*real* relationships.

Clearly Emma is not interested in real relationships of any kind – what she wants is the kind of adultery you read about in Harlequin Romances, the steamy affairs that never lose their risqué qualities and over-the-top passions. For this reason, Emma ends up just being an annoying mistress to both of her lovers; they're irritated by her carping demands, and by her childish view of love.

However, we're forgetting the thing that makes it possible for Emma go blundering through life as well as she does – she's *gorgeous*. Her beauty is really her greatest asset, and it allows people to forgive her time and time again for her mistakes. She's also charming and quite charismatic when she wants to be…she just doesn't always want to be.

Emma the Financial Planner
This is by far the most infuriating aspect of Emma's personality. Her comprehension of commerce is truly abysmal, yet Charles, ever conciliatory, allows her to take care of their affairs. What? Really? However you add it up, Emma's money troubles are unavoidable. She makes matters worse by simply pretending that nothing's going on, which is never a good idea.

Emma Bovary Timeline and Summary

- We first see Emma at Les Bertaux, rather ineptly attempting to help with her father's broken leg.
- Charles keeps visiting Les Bertaux, supposedly to check on Monsieur Rouault, but really to check Emma out.
- After an un-chaperoned visit, in which Emma talks her head off and Charles sits and listens, the two get engaged.
- Emma wants a ridiculously romantic wedding at midnight, but her dad says no.
- The actual wedding is a big affair in village society, and all the guests gorge themselves. Emma returns to Tostes with Charles.
- We learn about Emma's past as a Catholic schoolgirl.
- Emma begins to feel unhappy about her marriage – she wonders if she was ever in love at

Madame Bovary
Shmoop Learning Guide

all.
- She gets a puppy, Djali, who becomes her closest companion.
- Emma impresses a local aristocrat and he invites the Bovarys to a ball.
- At the La Vaubyessard ball, Emma gets her first taste of the good life – she's infatuated by it.
- After the ball, she can't stop thinking about her contact with wealth.
- Emma starts to obsess over the idea of Parisian life. She creates an exotic imaginary world populated by rich and beautiful lords and ladies.
- At this stage, Emma is a good housewife – she impresses Charles with her redecoration of the house and her little touches here and there. Her habits are somewhat expensive, but he doesn't care.
- Emma, however, gets more and more irritated with her husband, and with her life in general. She falls into a depression and suffers from uncontrollable mood swings.
- Charles, distraught, decides to move away from Tostes, in the hopes that Emma will recover.
- As they leave, we discover that Emma is pregnant.
- The new town, Yonville-l'Abbaye, is indeed larger than Tostes, but that's not exactly saying much. It's still a smallish market town, not far from Rouen.
- The Bovarys' arrival in Yonville isn't very fortuitous – Djali the dog is lost.
- Emma meets Léon Dupuis, a young clerk, and the two quickly become friends. They're both interested in books, music, and art.
- Emma gives birth to a baby girl (she's disappointed, since she'd wanted a boy). She can't decide upon a name, and eventually chooses Berthe.
- Emma realizes first that Léon is in love with her, and then that she is in love with him. She builds up a new fantasy life with him at the center.
- At home, things get worse and worse. Emma can't stand Charles, and her discontent explodes into rage. She attempts to resolve her issues by playing the role of the good wife, and even goes to talk to Father Bournisien, in an attempt to slough off her spiritual angst. It doesn't work.
- When Léon moves away, Emma's fantasies are shattered. Once again, her emotions spiral out of control.
- Charles asks his mother for advice – the older woman comes to visit, and antagonizes her daughter-in-law rather than helping. She thinks Emma reads too many novels, which are supposedly corrupting her.
- Just when things are at their nadir, a new man comes into Emma's life – Rodolphe Boulanger.
- Emma impresses Rodolphe with her beauty and utility; she helps Charles with a blood-letting procedure and doesn't faint.
- Yonville throws a big agricultural fair, and Rodolphe escorts Emma around the exhibits. He's at the top of his flirting game, and Emma falls for his poor-little-rich-man act.
- After the fair, Rodolphe convinces Charles to let Emma go horseback riding. Emma resists for a brief while, perhaps knowing the danger of going anywhere with Rodolphe, but gives in when told she can order a new riding outfit.
- Rodolphe and Emma set out for the woods, and Emma observes Yonville from a distance with disgust.
- In the woods, Rodolphe leads Emma to a secluded glade and declares his love for her. She resists at first, but quickly surrenders herself, body and soul, to him.

Madame Bovary
Shmoop Learning Guide

- Emma feels like a different woman. She's an adulteress, and is proud of it. She feels as though she has attained a higher, almost mythical state of being.
- Emma starts to spend money recklessly, pushing extravagant gifts on Rodolphe. Monsieur Lheureux keeps pushing her to buy more, and she borrows money from him to pay for it.
- Enamored, Emma gives in totally to her passion for Rodolphe, even taking rather absurd risks to visit him at his chateau in the early mornings.
- Rodolphe warns Emma that she's getting too careless. She begins to worry about being discovered.
- The two lovers find a new meeting place, in the secluded garden behind the Bovary house.
- Emma and Rodolphe's affair begins to cool down. She starts to feel guilty, and even attempts to love her little daughter more. She wonders why she can't love Charles.
- Speaking of which, Homais tells Emma about a new treatment available for clubfeet. The two of them decide that Charles should undertake this operation on a local clubfoot, Hippolyte. Charles gives in and says he'll do it.
- Emma gets excited about the prospect of this operation, which could potentially bring Charles fame and renown. She begins to cautiously warm up to her husband.
- Unfortunately, the operation is a disaster, and Hippolyte ends up with his leg amputated, rather than cured. Emma's disgust for Charles returns.
- Emma runs back to Rodolphe's arms, and they start up their affair with renewed vigor.
- Things intensify, and Emma convinces Rodolphe that they should run away together. She totally believes that it's going to happen, but he has major, *major* doubts.
- Rodolphe's doubts win in the end, and he writes Emma a totally sappy break-up letter on the same day they're supposed to elope.
- Emma falls into her worst depression yet – it's so profound that it destroys her emotionally and physically.
- After a slow recovery, Homais suggests that Charles take Emma to Rouen to see the opera, hoping that it'll cheer her up.
- Unfortunately, the opera is *Lucia di Lammermoor*, a cheery little diversion about a heroine that goes mad when forced to marry a man she doesn't love. This hits a little too close to home.
- However, some good does come from this outing for Emma – she and Charles run into Léon, who's done with law school, and returned to Rouen a man of the world. They leave the theatre early to go and talk.
- Léon convinces Charles that Emma should stay in Rouen for an extra day to see the end of the opera. We know that he *really* wants her to stay to hang out with him…
- Léon shows up at Emma's hotel the next day to woo her. They admit their love for each other, but Emma attempts to hold herself back. That evening, she decides to break things off with Léon before they even start, and writes him an explanatory letter.
- However, she delivers said letter herself, and gets entangled with Léon all over again. They meet in the cathedral at Rouen, and after a comical tour given by an over-determined guide, the couple gets in a horse-drawn cab to, er, work out their differences.
- We can only guess what happens inside the cab as it drives around all day. It's obvious by the end of it that Emma and Léon are now an item.
- Emma hurries back to Yonville, and is told to go next door to the pharmacy. There, she is met by a big to-do in the Homais household. Justin almost accidentally used a jar contaminated with arsenic for jam, and Monsieur Homais is totally enraged. Emma discovers the whole family panicking in the closet where the poisons are kept.

Madame Bovary
Shmoop Learning Guide

- In the hustle and bustle, Monsieur Homais bluntly tells her that her father-in-law is dead.
- Emma returns home to find Charles, distraught. Instead of being sympathetic, she's impatient with him; she wants to be alone so she can think about her new affair.
- Monsieur Lheureux arrives to discuss the many loans that the Bovarys have taken out. He ends up selling some more items to Emma, thus increasing the loans rather than decreasing them.
- Lheureux convinces Emma to talk to Charles about gaining power of attorney, which would give her the right to control the couple's financial matters.
- Emma brings the power of attorney up with Charles, who agrees, and then goes to Rouen, supposedly to talk to Léon about the contract.
- Emma remains in Rouen for three days, enjoying her time with her new lover.
- To enable her visits to Rouen, Emma becomes a master liar. She tells Charles that she goes into town every Thursday for piano lessons. Her time with Léon is the highlight of each week.
- Emma's lies grow more and more convoluted, as she has to explain why she doesn't come home one Thursday.
- Finances continue to get worse. Lheureux convinces Emma to let him handle the sale of a small property that Charles's father left in his will. Despite the money from the sale, Emma is up to her ears in debt, but she continues to spend glibly. She doesn't have the patience to figure out exactly how much she owes.
- Things with Léon start to cool off, especially after one Thursday in which he fails to meet her at their hotel room – Monsieur Homais is in town to visit for a day, and won't let Léon get away.
- One day, all of Emma's chickens come home to roost – Monsieur Lheureux decides that its time to cash in on all of her debts. She manages to put him off for a while, and does everything she can to earn some money. She attempts to sell all of her beautiful things, but it's no use. She even forces Léon to pawn some spoons her father gave her for her wedding.
- After a long, debauched night of partying in Rouen with Léon and his friends, Emma realizes just how low she has sunk – the other women present are prostitutes.
- Horrified, Emma rushes home. Her repentance is too late, though; Lheureux has had her property seized. She owes eight thousand francs, to be delivered in the next twenty four hours.
- Emma desperately tries to get the money from everyone she knows – Léon, Monsieur Guillaumin (the town notary), even Rodolphe. Everyone rejects her.
- Defeated, Emma rushes home. On her way back, she stops at the pharmacy, where she forces Justin to open the closet with all the poisons for her. Determined to die, she eats rat poison as Justin watches in horror. She threatens to blame him if he tells.
- Emma goes home and calmly writes a suicide note explaining her actions.
- After a while, the poison kicks in. Emma vomits profusely, and is wracked with pain. Charles doesn't know what to do.
- Emma's condition worsens, and real doctors are summoned. However, it's too late – there's nothing to be done.
- Emma realizes as she lies dying that Charles truly loves her, as nobody else has.
- Emma dies.

Madame Bovary
Shmoop Learning Guide

Charles Bovary Character Analysis

Charles is really just a normal guy. He's neither good nor bad; his biggest faults are simply that he's wishy-washy and not so bright. He can't even conceive of ever being dishonest himself, and therefore he never suspects anyone else of being dishonest to him. On the positive side, he's incredibly loyal, sweet, and supremely forgiving. This is all that Charles ever aspires to be. Under the right circumstances, Charles might have had a pretty nice life.

Unfortunately, Charles just married the wrong woman (or women). We get the feeling that in some alternate universe, he might have ended up with a sweet, easy-going woman who would be perfectly happy with the life before her. They would never fight, and never, ever even think about cheating on each other. Life would be terrific – not exciting, not adventurous, but incredibly pleasant and consistent. We can't help but wish that this life could have happened for Charles.

What *does* befall Charles is truly heartbreaking. First of all, the guy goes from a domineering mother to a domineering first wife, to a domineering *second* wife. Sure, he really should have more of a backbone – but in the long run, he really just doesn't want to hurt anyone's feelings. He loves the two main women in his life, Emma and his mother, *so* much that he can't separate his judgments from his emotions. Yes, he's foolish, but you know what? He's really not a bad guy, and he doesn't deserve what comes to him.

Sure, we get angry with Charles, and yes, we can understand what drives Emma crazy about him. He is, after all, a creature entirely devoid of ambition. He is also a pretty bad father to poor little Berthe once Emma dies. All in all, though, Charles's whole mode of operation is just to love and be loved – and, once his undeserving true love, Emma, dies, he has no choice but to fade away.

Charles Bovary Timeline and Summary

- Charles Bovary shows up at boarding school in Rouen – he's notable only for his work ethic and his horrendous fashion sense.
- Charles goes on to medical school to become an *officier de santé* (a sort of junior doctor). He fails his exams at first, having squandered his time in the tavern, but passes on the second go.
- Madame Bovary Sr. marries her son off to an unattractive, demanding, and supposedly wealthy widow. The couple takes up residence in the small town of Tostes.
- Charles splints Monsieur Rouault's broken leg at Les Bertaux, and meets Emma there.
- Thinking of Emma, Charles returns to the farm time and time again to visit with father and daughter.
- Charles's wife complains about this, knowing that there's another woman involved. Before long, however, she dies.
- Charles and Emma have some alone time one day, after which Charles resolves to marry her.

Madame Bovary
Shmoop Learning Guide

- The engagement is soon set – Monsieur Rouault loves Charles, and Emma thinks she does, too.
- Charles and Emma are married at Les Bertaux, and a whole passel of family and friends descends upon the house.
- After the wedding, the young couple moves to Charles's house in Tostes.
- Charles is impressed and pleased with Emma's changes to the house. He *does* feel torn between his wife and his mother, who doesn't approve of Emma, and is secretly just jealous that Charles loves her more.
- Charles gives in to Emma's every whim, even when her whims are expensive. He's just tickled pink by his wife, and can't believe his luck. Little does he know what Emma really thinks of him…
- After attending the ball at La Vaubyessard and Emma's subsequent depression, Charles consults with his mother and former teacher. They decide that a change of scenery would be good for Emma, so Charles finds a new post in Yonville.
- The pair moves to Yonville as Emma prepares for the birth of their child.
- Charles is unhappy in the new town, since he has no patients and few friends. Monsieur Homais quickly becomes his closest companion.
- Homais and Emma convince Charles that he should undertake the clubfoot surgery. He attempts to learn the ins and outs of the procedure.
- Operating upon Hippolyte, Charles makes a terrible mistake – he simply slices through the Achilles tendon, thinking that it's the right thing to do.
- It's not. Hippolyte's club foot is not cured, and it gets horrifically infected. A real doctor, Monsieur Canivet, has to be called in to amputate the foot.
- Charles is mortified and ashamed. He feels bad every time he hears Hippolyte's wooden leg clicking towards him on the street.
- Charles gets over this embarrassment fairly quickly. He's still desperately in love with Emma, and is infatuated with their child, Berthe. He envisions a future in which the family is loving and happy.
- After Emma is dumped by Rodolphe, Charles is forced to handle the couple's financial troubles. He signs more promissory notes with Lheureux, getting them deeper into debt.
- Charles fails to see that Emma is cheating on him. He glibly goes about his business, thinking that everything is peachy keen.
- On the day that Emma doesn't come home, Charles goes mad with worry. He goes to Rouen to find her but, when he does, he immediately believes her cock and bull story about feeling ill, and gives her even greater license to run off with his permission.
- When the property is seized, Charles is totally taken by surprise. He panics when he can't find Emma anywhere.
- The arsenic begins to act on Emma, and Charles doesn't know what to do. He freaks out when he can't figure out her symptoms, and writes urgently to Canivet and Doctor Larivière.
- Monsieur Homais, Canivet, and Larivière all attempt to help Emma, but it's pointless – the poison has already done its work. She dies; Charles is in a state of total despair.
- Charles plans an expensive and romantic funeral for his beloved wife. When his mother complains about the expense, he finally stands up to her for the first time in his life.
- After the funeral, Charles's life never returns to normal. He misses Emma ridiculously and still loves her, even after he discovers her adulterous relationship with Rodolphe.
- He begins to waste money on things that Emma would have liked, sinking deeper yet into

Madame Bovary
Shmoop Learning Guide

debt.
- After the elder Madame Bovary offers to take care of Berthe, Charles and his mother quarrel and break off their relationship again, this time for good.
- Charles loses his faith in God, and loses touch with the other townspeople.
- Charles stops seeing patients, and can't care for himself or for Berthe. He grows more and more jealous of Homais, who seems to have everything he ever wanted.
- One day, Charles and Rodolphe encounter each other. They awkwardly have a drink together; Charles ends by saying that he doesn't blame Rodolphe for Emma's adultery – only fate.
- Still lovelorn, Charles dies at home, clutching a lock of Emma's hair.

Monsieur Homais Character Analysis

Homais is a middle-class businessman at heart, but his ambitions never let him stop climbing the social ladder. He strives to be something more than just middle-class, and he attempts to pose as a cultured man to give himself an air of refinement. He's an unstoppable networker, and always has time to talk with someone important; even in the middle of Emma's gruesome death throes, Homais has the presence of mind to invite the two visiting doctors, Canivet and Larivière, over to his house for an extravagant lunch.

We get the feeling that he's a nice guy as long as you're on his side – however, when you're not, he's *ruthless*. And trust us, you don't want to be on Monsieur Homais's bad side. His relentless brown-nosing gets him places, and he ends the novel as a tremendously influential man. When he receives the Cross of the Legion of Honor in the novel's closing line, all of his ambitions are fulfilled – and characteristically, he achieves this last honor simply by sucking up to the right people and talking himself up.

Monsieur Homais Timeline and Summary

- Homais greets Emma and Charles as they arrive in Yonville. He's determined to keep Charles on his side, since he's been threatened with legal action after being caught practicing medicine illegally.
- Homais becomes the young couples' best friend; he visits constantly and is always trying to make himself useful.
- Homais tells Emma about the clubfoot surgery, and the two of them convince Charles to do it.
- Homais also convinces Hippolyte the clubfoot, the other essential party to this operation, to undergo the surgery.
- After the operation, Homais writes it up for a Rouen newspaper, exaggerating the details to miraculous proportions. Of course, he makes no mention of the actual disastrous outcome.
- During Emma's slow recovery from her abandonment by Rodolphe, Homais suggests that Charles take her to the theatre. The pharmacist gets into a rousing argument with Father

Madame Bovary
Shmoop Learning Guide

Bournisien about literature, music, and theatre.
- On jam-making day, Homais gets angry with Justin for letting the arsenic jar get dangerously close to the jam. Still enraged, he tells Emma that her father-in-law is dead, forgetting to make the speech he'd planned.
- Homais visits Léon in Rouen, occupying him all day while the young man keeps trying to get to his rendezvous with Emma.
- On the day of Emma's mad flight around Rouen and Yonville, Homais runs into her in the Hirondelle. He has been buying rolls for his wife in Rouen. He yells at the blind beggar about bogus cures he should be taking for his eyes.
- Homais tries to help Charles take care of Emma, but has nothing productive to offer.
- When Dr. Larivière arrives, Homais invites him and Monsieur Canivet over for lunch.
- Homais invents a cover-up for Emma's suicide, saying that she accidentally consumed the arsenic.
- After Emma's death, Homais delicately separates his family from Charles and Berthe. Before then, though, he helps Charles pick an extravagant gravestone for Emma.
- Homais immerses himself in civic life, attempting to procure the Medal of the Legion of Honor.
- Homais has the blind beggar, his arch-nemesis, locked up forever in an asylum.
- He also starts work on a book on Yonville.
- When other doctors attempt to move into Yonville after Charles's death, Homais basically chases them out of town. He has a monopoly on the medical trade in the town.
- All of Monsieur Homais's ambitions and dreams are fulfilled, except for the Legion of Honor.
- As the novel ends, he finally attains this goal.

Rodolphe Boulanger de la Huchette Character Analysis

Rodolphe is another fairly recognizable stock character – he's a handsome, skilled Casanova, whose only goal in life is to woo women. He decides immediately upon meeting Emma that she should be his next mistress. Even at that early point, he knows that their affair will end when he's sick of it; he contemplates how to escape from their relationship before it even begins.

We know Rodolphe is bad news, not just because he's untrustworthy, but because of how hard Emma falls for him. He's everything she's ever wanted – rich, handsome, smooth, and apparently sensitive (or at least, she thinks he is).

With all of these appealing traits, however, come some less savory characteristics. We are told that Rodolphe has "a brutal temperament and a shrewd intelligence" (II.7.34), a dangerous combination. He has the casual apathy of the rich classes – a downside to wealth that Emma never considers – and treats women with the same indifference as he treats his objects. Emma is no different. Sure, he cares for her and is infatuated by her beauty, but ultimately, Rodolphe is unwilling to change his life for her. He lives a profoundly selfish existence, and doesn't care about the people he hurts along the way.

Madame Bovary
Shmoop Learning Guide

Rodolphe Boulanger de la Huchette Timeline and Summary

- Rodolphe meets Emma at the Bovary house, when his servant has to be bled.
- Emma immediately impresses him with her elegance and beauty, as well as her steady head during the bleeding.
- That's it – Rodolphe decides that Emma will be his next mistress. He doesn't even wonder if she'll say no. It's inconceivable, apparently.
- At the town fair, Emma and Rodolphe take a walk together. He launches into a long spiel about how very sad and lonely he is, and how hard it is to be him. This is totally Emma's kind of thing – we're amazed by Rodolphe's skill with the ladies. And we're nervous.
- Rodolphe convinces Charles that Emma should go out horseback riding.
- The next day, Rodolphe and Emma go for a ride in the woods. Rodolphe leads her to a secluded glade and declares his love for her. Emma resists – but very quickly abandons herself to him.
- Rodolphe enjoys the affair for a while. He's charmed by Emma's beauty and innocence, and seems to actually care about her.
- Things wind down a little bit as time goes on, and the two fall into a pattern that resembles dull married life rather than thrilling adulterous adventures.
- After the clubfoot debacle, Emma gives up on her attempt to be a good wife and runs back to Rodolphe.
- Their affair intensifies after this point. Rodolphe is alternately irritated and amused by the romantic things Emma makes him do – she plies him with gifts, makes him swear oaths, and even wants to have wedding rings. Most importantly, she thinks they're running away together.
- Rodolphe, not one to spoil the fun, lets Emma believe that they will actually run off. They even pick a date. When the day comes, Rodolphe puts it off for longer…and longer. Finally, a definitive plan is made for their escape from Yonville.
- When the day comes, though, Rodolphe can't do it. He's horrified by the idea of saddling himself not just with a woman, but with a child (Berthe). He writes a melodramatic note to Emma, and even adds fake teardrops.
- We don't see Rodolphe again until the end of the book. Emma comes to him to ask for the thousands of francs she owes Lheureux; first, she acts as though she wants to get back together with him (which almost works – he still has some feelings for her). When he finds out it's just about the money, though, he sends her away. We're told that if he had that much cash available, he would give it to her – which we believe.
- After Emma's death, Rodolphe has an awkward encounter with Charles. They have a drink, and Charles says that he doesn't hold anything against Rodolphe – he thinks it was fate. Rodolphe doesn't buy this, and leaves the bar thinking that Charles is pathetic.

Léon Dupuis Character Analysis

When first we meet him, Léon is kind of the male equivalent of Emma. He's young, attractive, idealistic, and romantic to a fault. He's also incredibly bored with small-town life in Yonville, and

Madame Bovary
Shmoop Learning Guide

looks forward to the day when he can escape to Paris to pursue his law degree. Léon is initially a young man with dreams of romance and love, but is totally inactive – he's afraid to tell Emma that he loves her, and instead pines after her until he leaves Yonville.

After he returns from Paris, however, Léon is a different animal. His experience with the worldly women of the capital have removed the veils of his tender fantasies; he no longer dreams delicately of his beautiful, untouchable passion for Emma. Now, Léon isn't satisfied with awkward flirtation. When reunited with Emma in Rouen, he goes straight in for the kill, flattering her with tales of his lovelorn misery, and inwardly plotting his conquest. Like Emma, Léon gradually loses his fairytale illusions, but never loses his desires – and like her, we get the feeling by the end of the novel that life has sullied and corrupted him.

Léon Dupuis Timeline and Summary

- Léon, a boarder at Monsieur Homais's house, meets Emma upon the Bovarys' arrival in Yonville.
- Emma and Léon chat it up all night, and the young man is flattered and infatuated with the doctor's wife.
- Léon has never experienced this kind of intimate conversation with a woman, and he's fascinated by Emma.
- After the birth of Emma's child, she and Léon take a walk to visit the baby (who's staying outside town with a wetnurse). The town is scandalized by how much time the two young people spend together.
- Emma and Léon are totally BFFs. He gets her little gifts like houseplants, and in return she has a beautiful blanket sent to him.
- Léon is head-over-heels in love with Emma, but he's too scared to do anything.
- Emma realizes that Léon is in love with her, which in turn makes her fall in love with him. She focuses all of her fantasies on him. However, in an attempt to turn her thoughts away from adultery, she tries to play the part of the virtuous good wife.
- Everyone is fooled by Emma's act, even Léon. Depressed and emotionally frustrated, he decides to leave for Paris earlier than planned. He pays Emma one last visit, in which he doesn't declare his love – instead, he makes a big show of saying goodbye to little Berthe.
- Léon heads off to law school in Paris for a couple of years, during which we don't see him. We learn later that he spends a lot of this time playing around with the ladies. He's a different man when he gets back.
- After his studies end, Léon moves back to Rouen.
- In Rouen, Léon has a chance encounter with Charles and Emma at the opera.
- Upon their reunion, all of the old feelings come rushing back again. Léon convinces Charles to let Emma stay in Rouen for an extra day to see the end of the opera (they left early).
- The next day, Léon goes to see Emma, after confirming that Charles headed back to Yonville. He visits her in her hotel room, where they talk openly about their feelings for the first time. However, both of them paint a deceptive picture of their time apart – Léon doesn't mention any other women, and Emma doesn't mention Rodolphe.

- The couple meets at the famous Rouen cathedral the next day. Emma is resolved to break off their affair before it even starts, but Léon has other ideas. After a hectic tour of the cathedral, they get in a cab.
- We don't see what happens in the cab, but we can imagine. They force the poor horse and driver to run around town all day so that they can have clandestine conversation (and other activities) in the secluded carriage. By the end of the day, they are clearly a couple.
- From this time on, Emma and Léon are an item. She comes to visit him in Rouen every week, and he even comes to visit in Yonville.
- In Rouen, the couple has a specific room at the luxurious Hôtel de Boulogne that they rent every Thursday. Emma pampers her lover, who basks in her attention.
- Léon gets in trouble at work for missing so many days because of Emma's visits. He keeps bowing to her whims, however, and skips out on work for her. He even does silly things like dress all in black and copy out love poems for her. He's confused by her wild behavior, but still intrigued by her.
- One day, Monsieur Homais comes to give Léon a surprise visit. Unfortunately, it's on one of Emma's Rouen days. The pharmacist irritatingly follows Léon around and prevents him from meeting Emma. In a huff, she leaves.
- After the Homais debacle, things start to slow down. Both Emma and Léon lose steam, and their affair gets less exciting. Léon starts to become less and less interested in Emma's affections.
- Emma keeps working at the relationship, hoping to feel something more exciting and genuine by throwing herself at him. Léon resents her dominant attitude, but she still has control over him.
- Léon begins to wonder if his mother (who heard a rumor about his mistress) and friends are right – should he get rid of Emma?
- Léon and Emma go to a masked ball with some of his friends, then spend all night partying. Emma realizes that she has sunk to new lows – all of Léon's pals are out with prostitutes.
- Léon and Emma are through. However, she does come and ask him desperately for the money she owes Lheureux. She attempts to force him to steal money from his office to give to her, or to take out promissory notes of his own. Léon says no, but lacks the will power to flat out refuse her. He half-heartedly goes out, but returns empty handed. Finally, to get rid of her, he tells her that a rich friend is coming back to town that night, and that he will meet her in Yonville the next day with the money. It's obviously a lie.
- Léon doesn't show the next day.
- After Emma's death, Léon ends up marrying someone else, and settles down to a quiet life as a notary in another town.

Monsieur Lheureux Character Analysis

Monsieur Lheureux is the closest thing we get to a truly evil creature. He is remorseless and cunning; he knows all along that he will drive Emma to financial ruin, and furthermore, he does it on purpose. When first we meet him, we learn that he has already driven another unfortunate citizen out of business and out of town (Madame Lefrançois's rival, the tavern keeper), and clearly, he has no qualms about doing the same to Emma. He even has the gall to show up at her funeral and look sad, even while he's pumping Charles for more cash. Lheureux shows us depths of depravity to which people can sink in the pursuit of money.

Berthe Bovary Character Analysis

Berthe doesn't do anything in particular, except show the faults of her parents. She's an infant, then a small child in the novel, and she simply is not old enough to act. However, we learn a great deal about both Charles and Emma through their interactions with her. Emma's love/hate relationship with the little girl plays up her own insecurities and fears, while Charles's loving neglect of Berthe at the end of the novel reveals his inability to care for himself, much less for another living being. As the novel ends, we perhaps feel the worst for poor Berthe, consigned to a life of poverty in the workhouse, who did nothing to deserve her tragic fate.

Madame Homais Character Analysis

Madame Homais is barely even a character. She's another young-ish housewife (she's in her thirties), but she couldn't be any more different from Emma. She's totally devoted to her husband's mission of getting ahead in life, and she doesn't really seem to have any other ambitions. She doesn't really care about her appearance or about how the outside world perceives her; she mostly stays at home and haphazardly takes care of the brood of unfortunately-named Homais kids. We don't really know anything about Madame Homais beyond her actions – she has no internal life, as far as we're concerned.

Character Roles

Protagonist
Emma Bovary
This is a no-brainer. Emma is the center of the novel's world, and she is the only character we see in such depth and realistic detail. She is the novel's protagonist, but notably *not* its heroine; this is a book without heroics of any kind. We see her actions, but are not asked to judge them…rather, we follow her through life, watching as she makes mistake after mistake. Yes, this perspective can be frustrating, but it's also fascinating. We know her more intimately than any of the other characters, and Flaubert fleshes her out to a far greater extent. By the end of the book, Emma is almost real to us; once she's gone, we feel the gaping hole left in the book, and in the lives of its characters.

Antagonist
Charles Bovary
Poor Charles. He certainly never meant to antagonize anyone, especially not Emma. However, try though he might to just get along with everyone, he still drives her craaaaazy. Without even knowing it, he becomes Emma's greatest enemy; she blames him for pretty much everything,

Madame Bovary
Shmoop Learning Guide

including even meeting her. Charles's doglike affection just serves to increase Emma's animosity, and it's as though the more he loves her, the more she despises him. In her eyes, he is the embodiment of all that's dull, commonplace, and confining about small-town life – and furthermore, it's his *fault* that she's stuck there.

Antagonist
Monsieur Homais
Homais basically antagonizes everyone in the town, including Charles and Emma (though they don't know it). His self-serving actions often entail negative consequences for everyone else, and he simply doesn't care – he just wants to get his way. He ran the previous doctor out of town, and after Charles, he does the same to the new doctors who try to set up practices in Yonville. With Charles, Homais simply tolerates his presence because he *must* – threatened with legal action, he has to keep the new doctor on his side. He manages to do this by playing the conscientious neighbor act, but his true colors emerge when he ditches Emma's deathbed to play host to the two big shot doctors, Canivet and Larivière.

Guide/Mentor
Monsieur Lheureux
Monsieur Lheureux certainly guides Emma – but *not* in a good way! Rather than being a mentor, he's a tempter. He's the Serpent to her Eve, and the temptations of his wares are ultimately what drive Emma to ruin. He manipulates her and teaches her all the wrong things about finances, and his training sets Emma up for disaster. She's a willing pupil – basically, Emma wants to believe everything that sounds like it'll get her what she wants. Lheureux knows exactly how to convince Emma, and he plans her financial downfall from the very beginning.

Foil
Madame Homais
Madame Homais is everything Emma is not – she devotes her whole life to her brood of oddly-named children, to her husband, and to his career. She's a character who's practically not even her own person; we don't know anything about her personal desires, likes, or dislikes (except for the fact that she loves the rolls Monsieur Homais brings back from the bakery in Rouen). She takes all her cues from her husband, and thus is perfectly suited to being the wife of such an ambitious and forceful man. The constant presence of Madame Homais right next door highlights Emma's own forceful disposition, and the power of her desires over her familial and social obligations.

Romantic Interest
Léon
Léon is sort of the best and worst possible romantic interest for Emma. They develop along parallel paths – when they meet, both are young, idealistic, and foolishly romantic, but when they are reunited in Rouen, both have been around the block once or twice. At the beginning of their actual affair, Emma has already been through her first romantic adventure with Rodolphe, and Léon has gained some experience with the prostitutes of Paris. This is both good and bad; while Léon can understand Emma's feelings and desires, they are perhaps too similar, which is why their affair can't last.

Madame Bovary
Shmoop Learning Guide

Romantic Interest
Rodolphe
It's quite possible that Rodolphe's sole purpose in this world is to get it on with the ladies. He's rich, handsome, lazy, super-masculine, and smooth as butter – and despite (or rather because) of all of this, Emma totally falls for his lame "sensitive guy" act. He has a specific function in the plot, which is simply to lure Emma into adultery, and thus start her on the path towards her tragic fate.

Character Clues

Social Class
This is a book about the middle class: none of its characters are either poverty-stricken or fantastically hoity-toity. Even Rodolphe, the richest character, is not exactly an aristocrat. Instead, he is simply a well-to-do guy, who still has bourgeois sensibilities. Flaubert is careful to show us all elements of the middle-class condition; we have Homais, who strives to rise above his class; Charles, who's content with what he has; Emma, who longs to be a great lady; and Léon, who's discontented but inactive. In showing us the troubles of the bourgeoisie, Flaubert paints a portrait of a very specific class at a very specific time in history.

Thoughts and Opinions
Flaubert takes us straight into the minds of our characters, revealing everything they think and feel to us. This is our best resource for getting to know them; he's unflinching and direct in showing us their deepest desires. We also hear a lot of opinions from characters like Homais and Father Bournisien. Rather than learning anything from the words spewing from Homais's mouth (most of which are kind of nonsense anyway), we learn a lot about his personality from the arrogant way in which he holds forth.

Actions
Actions do indeed speak louder than words here. We see characters say one thing and do another over and over again, thus betraying their real personalities. The first example that springs to mind is Homais's abandonment of Emma's deathbed; he chooses to take the doctors to lunch at his house to try and curry favor with them, instead of staying with his supposed friend, Charles, in his moment of need. We might also look to Rodolphe, who keeps reassuring Emma that he will run away with her, but actually balks at the last minute, and instead runs away by himself. We can only judge the characters by what they do, rather than what they say.

Names
Many of the names in *Madame Bovary* comment aptly upon the nature of the characters. "Bovary," for example, is a play on "bovine," or cow-like. That is indeed what Charles is – he's a placid herd animal, who's always willing to go along with the status quo. Notably, Rodolphe comments on how everyone calls Emma by that name, but it's not hers. Monsieur Homais's name also offers some commentary upon him; it sounds unmistakably like the French words "homme, mais," which translate to "a man, but..." Homais is exactly that; he's certainly a real guy, but he also has some startlingly inhuman traits. Finally, Lheureux, or "l'heureux," means

Madame Bovary
Shmoop Learning Guide

"happy man" in French, which is just what the money-lending merchant is – his gazillions of francs give him joy, despite the sorrow he causes.

Literary Devices

Symbols, Imagery, Allegory

Emma's appearance
The more Emma transgresses, the more beautiful she grows – as though her body responds to the corruption of her soul. Emma's beauty reaches its greatest height at the end of the novel, as she commits her worst crime, suicide.

Why should this happen, though? What does Emma's appearance signify? There's no absolute answer to that, but we think it has to do with her intense connection to her physicality. As Emma delves deeper into her desires, indulging more and more in sensuality, her body becomes far more present, both to us, the readers, and to Emma herself. As she gives in to her long-repressed physical desires, her body flourishes and her beauty exerts more power.

The Blind Man
The image of the blind beggar occurs several times as the novel nears its end. Emma first feels something akin to pity towards him, but her feelings are always tinged with disgust. His appearance represents the intensifying corruption of Emma's soul, and as her situation worsens, he shows up more and more frequently. It's notable that his horrifying physical appearance is described with the same kind of obsessive detail usually reserved to describe Emma's beauty; we have distinct mental images of both Emma and the beggar, but really not of anyone else. This sets the two of them and links them in our minds.

The presence of the blind man at the scene of Emma's death is particularly disturbing. Emma is profoundly upset by the sound of his harsh voice outside her window as she lies dying, and the end of his song comes at the same moment that Emma dies. Fittingly, the last line of the song tells us that the woman in it was no innocent young lady, but was instead a strumpet who lost her petticoat. This rude ending aligns to Emma's own unfortunate end; while the song's closing line is comical, it comments grimly upon the very un-funny closing of Emma's life.

Setting

Tostes, Yonville-l'Abbaye, and Rouen, France
Unlike many of the other famous French novels of the nineteenth century that you might encounter (such as Victor Hugo's *Les Misérables* or Honoré de Balzac's *Père Goriot*), which more often than not take place in the booming, magical, romantic metropolis of Paris, *Madame Bovary* is planted firmly in the French provinces. This is actually a significant part of the novel; Emma, our heroine, spends much of her time lamenting the fact that she's stuck in the sleepy

Madame Bovary
Shmoop Learning Guide

little towns of Tostes and Yonville. The biggest city she ever gets to is Rouen, a smallish city famous primarily for its beautiful cathedral.

Emma's provincial surroundings make her feel even more trapped and unhappy in her marriage; she feels as though there's nothing to do but care for her home and child (which, for a woman, was pretty much true at that time). Emma has a feeling that she's *meant* for the big city, as though her beauty and charm are wasted in small towns. Rodolphe actually notes a similar thing, saying that she's as elegant as a fashionable Paris lady.

In the novel, Paris itself represents the culmination of all of Emma's dreams – she imagines that life there is everything she longs for it to be, with beautiful things, beautiful people, and beautiful feelings. What she has instead is dull small town life, and her bitterness about its limitations contributes largely to her discontent.

Narrator Point of View

Supposedly First Person; Actually Third Person Omniscient

This sounds quite odd and complicated, and it kind of is. In the first chapter, we have a mysterious, nameless, faceless first person narrator (supposedly a former classmate of Charles Bovary) who recounts the first time Charles appeared in boarding school. However, this is not your average first person narrator. We don't know anything about the guy, and he doesn't make a single appearance in the book. Furthermore, he knows *everything* about Charles. This makes for a natural transition into the narrative voice of the rest of the book; from Chapter Two on out, we see things through the perspective of a third person omniscient point of view. But again, this is not simply an average outside observer…we get a deeply personal, intensely internalized view of the characters.

The point of view of *Madame Bovary* was pretty radical when the novel came out. Flaubert delves way down into the psychological depths of his main character, and we emerge with a portrait of Emma that is unflinching in its directness. We can look at her objectively and be like, "You brought this all upon herself," but at the same time, we feel her pain; we experience what she experiences and understand why she makes the decisions that she does. We can see why Flaubert himself famously claimed, "Madame Bovary, c'est moi" (I am Madame Bovary). By the end of the book, we readers might also say, "We are Madame Bovary."

Genre

Realism

Madame Bovary was actually a big turning point for Flaubert. You see, he, like Emma, really loved the lush beauty of Romanticism, and even wrote his fair share of romantic tales. Even after *Madame Bovary*, he went back to the Romantic mode occasionally (notably with *Salammbô*). However, for this novel, the author's friends actually challenged him to write a

Madame Bovary
Shmoop Learning Guide

Realist novel, hoping to cure him of his Romantic inclinations – and it's a good thing they did. *Madame Bovary* is now regarded as one of the most important examples of this genre. The detail and psychological depth with which Flaubert shapes his characters has made this novel one of the most influential books ever written. For a guy who wasn't really that interested in Realism to begin with, Flaubert did a pretty amazing job.

Tone

Intimate Yet Detached
"Intimate yet detached" sounds paradoxical, but it's true. Flaubert's novel manages somehow to be both intimate and detached from its main characters – as though it can peer inside their souls, while still remaining outside ultimately. Flaubert accomplishes this by refusing to manipulate the reader's emotions; instead of getting us to sympathize with Emma or Charles, we see and understand what's going on with them, but don't get totally caught up in it ourselves.

A very powerful (and famous) example of this tone is Emma's death scene: we know what she's thinking and feeling, and we are certainly deeply affected by her torments, but we're not exactly weeping. When Flaubert describes her horrifying last moments, then ends with the masterfully dramatic, deceptively simple statement, "She had ceased to exist" (III.8.111), we can feel the power of death – the sudden absence of a person we know well. Yet we still remain outside of the scene, observing Charles' grief, but not feeling it as our own.

Writing Style

Alternately Ironic and Descriptive
Flaubert's style in this book is an interesting mish-mash of different elements. He's somehow able to combine straightforward, un-decorative irony with gorgeous, evocative description, and emerge with a text that's cohesive and totally unique – mad props to him.

We see killer one-liners that are devastating in their simplicity, in which the true ridiculousness of humanity is made glaringly obvious. (The most notable example is the last line: "He has just been awarded the Cross of the Legion of Honor.")

On the other hand, we also indulge in evocative moments of intimate detail, particularly relating to Emma's various states of being. For example, after her first physical experience with Rodolphe, we can almost feel "her heart beating again, and the blood flowing through her flesh like a river of milk" (II.9.49). Taken all together, the style of this book is both a reminder that we're human, and that, as humans, we're incredibly flawed.

Madame Bovary
Shmoop Learning Guide

What's Up With the Title?

This is pretty straightforward: *Madame Bovary* is about *Madame Bovary*. The novel falls in the tradition of books named after their heroes (think *David Copperfield*, *Oliver Twist*, *Emma*, *Jane Eyre*, etc.). However, Flaubert's novel threw in an inventive and perhaps unsettling twist – the eponymous Madame Bovary isn't exactly a heroine. Yes, she is our protagonist, and yes, she is the center of the novel. However, she doesn't awaken our sense of compassion or sympathy in the same way that the other characters listed above do (see more on this in "Character Role Identification"). Furthermore, the novel was condemned at the time of its publication for being too racy, and for not portraying the scandalous life and times of Emma Bovary in terms of morality. Flaubert did a gutsy thing when he decided to simply name his novel after this ambiguous and difficult character – the title places no judgment, and gives us no hint of how we are supposed to perceive her.

What's Up With the Epigraph?

[Dedication to Marie-Antoine-Jules Senard]

Dear and illustrious friend,
Allow me to inscribe your name at the head of this book and above its dedication, for it is to you, more than anyone else, that I owe its publication. In passing through your magnificent pleas in court, my work has acquired, in my eyes, a kind of unexpected authority. I therefore ask you to accept here the tribute of my gratitude, which, however great it may be, will never reach the height of your eloquence or your devotion.
– Gustave Flaubert

OK, you've got us – this is not actually an epigraph at all. Rather, it's a very significant dedication. We just couldn't figure out where else this very significant explanatory note could go. Anyway, the "illustrious" man to whom Flaubert is so very grateful is Marie-Antoine-Jules Senard (a guy, despite his first name). Senard was a big shot lawyer of the time and, when Flaubert was put on trial in 1857 for *Madame Bovary* (which was deemed too steamy for public consumption), Senard successfully defended him, saving both the novel and its author from big, big trouble. The novel, which gained notoriety through press coverage of the trial, went on to become a giant bestseller (looks like things haven't really changed since then).

What's Up With the Ending?

The end of *Madame Bovary* is classic Flaubert. Seriously, the guy just *loooved* a good ironic twist. Then again, who doesn't? Basically, the outlook is grim for basically all of the sympathetic characters of the book – Emma is dead, having succumbed to what is possibly the *worst death ever* (two words: rat poison!), Charles is also dead (broken heart), and poor little Berthe, the unfortunate daughter of the two, is a child laborer in a cotton mill. The one character that triumphs turns out to be the despicable Monsieur Homais, the social climbing apothecary. The novel ends with a single, infuriating declaration: "He has just been awarded the cross of the Legion of Honor."

Gaah – it doesn't matter how many times we've read it, this ending still just drives us crazy!

Madame Bovary
Shmoop Learning Guide

And we're *meant* to be driven crazy by it. By rewarding Homais with this honor, Flaubert cruelly underlines the series of depressingly unromantic points that the novel as a whole drives home: life is not fair; people can be lame; society is, more often then not, just flat-out *wrong*.

Finally, one more important thing to note is the change in tense here; Flaubert switches from the past tense to the present in the last couple of pages of the book. This brings the book directly into the world of the reader, and thus makes it more *real* to us, as though Berthe and Monsieur Homais are people out there in the world right now. Of course, the older the book gets, the less likely this is (unless these characters are *exceptionally* long-lived) – but still, you get the point.

Did You Know?

Trivia

- A 2007 book, *The Top Ten*, compiled best book ever lists from 125 famous authors – when an ultimate top ten was constructed out of these lists, *Madame Bovary* came in second! (Source)

Steaminess Rating

R
Madame Bovary is about as sexy as it gets in the world of nineteenth century novels. We're talking secret rendezvous in a moving cab, clandestine moonlit embraces, and – let's count 'em, folks – not just one, but TWO adulterous affairs in one three-hundred page book.

That being said, there are no actual sex scenes in this book – remember, this is steamy by stodgy nineteenth century standards. However, the very clear *suggestion* of sex was enough to get Flaubert put on trial for obscenity.

Allusions and Cultural References

Literature, Philosophy, and Mythology

- Jacques-Henri Bernardin de Saint-Pierre, *Paul et Virginie* (I.6.1)
- Sir Walter Scott (I.6.6; *Bride of Lammermoor*, II.15.6)
- Eugène Sue (I.9.6)
- Honoré de Balzac (I.9.6)

Madame Bovary
Shmoop Learning Guide

- George Sand (I.9.6)
- Voltaire (II.7.14; II.14.7; II.14.19, III.9.29)
- Baron d'Holbach (III.9.29)

Historical References

- French Revolution (I.6.6)
- Mary, Queen of Scots (I.6.6)
- Joan of Arc (I.6.6)
- Héloïse (I.6.6)
- Agnès Sorel (I.6.6)
- Clémence Isaure (I.6.6)
- Massacre of St. Bartholomew (I.6.6)
- Death of the Duke of Clarence (II.12.23)
- Louise de la Vallière (II.14.9)
- Louis XIII (III.V.104)

Pop Culture

- Leonardo da Vinci, *La Belle Ferronnière*, painting (I.6.6)
- Gaetano Donizetti, *Lucia di Lammermoor*, an opera (II.15.1)
- Charles Steuben, *Esmerelda*, painting (III.7.48)
- Henri-Frédéric Schopin, *Potiphar*, painting (III.7.48)

Best of the Web

Movie or TV Productions

2001 TV Version (UK)
http://www.imdb.com/title/tt0212318/
The most recent production of the novel.

1991 film (France)
http://www.imdb.com/title/tt0102368/
This is probably the most popular version, starring the great French actress Isabelle Huppert.

1949 film (US)
http://www.imdb.com/title/tt0041615/
Here's a 1949 version, directed by Vincente Minelli (father of Liza).

Madame Bovary
Shmoop Learning Guide

1933 film (France)
http://www.imdb.com/title/tt0025442/
This is the first *Madame Bovary* version to make it to the big screen!

Videos
1991 film trailer
http://www.youtube.com/watch?v=1cvXbHwpg90&feature=related
This trailer has a fascinating chocolate commercial vibe to it…we love it.

Images
Ah, Gustave!
http://www.cartoonstock.com/lowres/jna0029l.jpg
A particularly charming cartoon of Flaubert.

Emma and Charles
http://img5.allocine.fr/acmedia/medias/nmedia/18/65/02/76/18829109.jpg
An image from the 1991 film.

Emma and Admirers
http://home.hiwaay.net/~oliver/madameb1.jpg
An image from the classic 1949 film.

Websites
Madame Bovary online
http://www.gutenberg.org/etext/2413
Here's the link to the e-text at the illustrious Project Gutenberg site.

Flaubert Bio
http://great-writers.suite101.com/article.cfm/gustave_flaubert
The lowdown on our friend Flaubert…

Printed in Great Britain
by Amazon.co.uk, Ltd.,
Marston Gate.